NAVIGATING THE CENTURY

NAVIGATING THE CENTURY

A PERSONAL ACCOUNT OF ALTER COMPANY'S FIRST HUNDRED YEARS

by Bernard Goldstein with William Petre

THE HISTORY FACTORY

Library of Congress Cataloging in Publication Data

Goldstein, Bernard, 1929-
Navigating the Century

97-078032

ISBN 1-882771-02-8

Published by The History Factory
14140 Parke Long Court
Chantilly, Virginia 20151-1649
Printed in the United States of America

I dedicate this book to the future,
and to my grandchildren:

Michael
Josh
Marc
Nathan
Samantha
Lauren
Jeremy
Alex
Jesse

May they have as much fun
as I have had.

TABLE OF CONTENTS

Introduction

In 1951, at the age of twenty-two, I received a law degree from the University of Illinois and was admitted to the Iowa Bar. It proved a short career. I tell people that I'm the best lawyer in Iowa history, because I never lost a case or a client. True, I never won a case either, or had a client, because I never practiced law. Instead, I joined the Davenport, Iowa, scrap metal company that belonged to Frank R. Alter, my father-in-law.

I've never had a moment's regret about that choice. It has given me a truly exciting, rewarding, and *different* life. I've sold scrap to a Baton Rouge transsexual who kept a lion in his/her back yard, soaked my socks with champagne while christening a *Diamond Lady*, had a towboat named after me, and delivered hundreds of thousands of tons of scrap to Mexico's Altos Hornos. Though I learned early on that building casinos often required the moving of enormous bureaucratic mountains, in Colorado I actually had to move a real one. I've helped build a network of scrap yards, a barge line, and a transportation business. I've watched with some wonderment as Alter Company evolved from running towboats on the upper Mississippi, to casino boats in the Gulf, to cruise ships on the sea.

I co-founded the Quad City Propeller Club and have been involved in numerous other civic, religious, and charitable organizations. I've been voted a Businessman of the Year and named a Simon Wiesenthal honoree. I helped bring employment, wealth, and prosperity to thousands of Midwesterners, as well as people from Louisiana, Mississippi, Tennessee, and many other states. I've also been blessed with a fabulous family and wonderful friends. Whenever I used to complain to my wife Renee how hard it was to find good young managers to bring into the business, she used to reply that she was raising them as fast as she could—and to that end she has given us four terrific children. That said, I was the one who gave birth to the whole riverboat gaming industry. (And boy, did that bring tears to my eyes!)

And through it all, I've had a wonderful time.

Handing on the company to my own children, as Frank handed it on to Renee and me, has given me a chance to reflect on both my time with the company and Alter

Company itself. Frank Alter did not found Alter Company. In fact, it was founded in Davenport, Iowa, in 1898, a year before Frank was even born. The names of the founders are lost to us, but in 1900, Frank's uncle, Harry Alter, joined the young firm, and in 1905 Frank's father, Morris, also joined. The two brothers soon became joint proprietors and remained so for the following fifteen years.

But it was Frank, more than anyone, who was responsible for building the company into significance. I'm about the last person at Alter Company who worked closely with Frank, and this book, as much as being a celebration of our first hundred years, is my tribute to him. There are many other people I would like to thank as well: Chuck Smith, Gordon Jones, Jake Barnes, Dee Lesher, and Lois Hansen, who were my good friends as well as my colleagues; and all the people who worked in our yards over the years or drove our trucks, operated our cranes, crewed our boats, or staffed our casinos.

Andrew Carnegie, the founder of U.S. Steel, and at one time the world's richest man, used to remark that the greatest reason for his success was that he surrounded himself with people smarter than himself. I know exactly how he felt, and at Alter we have been fortunate to have enjoyed excellent advice from some of the finest lawyers, accountants, bankers, insurers, and other consultants imaginable, and have built extremely good relationships with them. There have been so many over the years that I can't list them all, but they include Alan Glazer, Dick Coonrod, Robert Ackerburg, Don Sitz, Don Decker, Bruno Valente, Dave Wentworth, and many, many others.

My appreciation also goes out to the broader world: to the inventors and entrepreneurs who made it possible to recycle scrap metal in gray iron foundries and open-hearth furnaces, and so gave rise to the scrap metal industry in the first place; to the Quad Cities, where I have lived and worked most of my life; and to the magnificent Mississippi River, which has affected so much of my life.

Finally, I guess there should be a word of thanks to those two vicious anti-Semites, Tsars Alexander III and Nicholas II, without whose tyrannical regimes Frank's family, my family, and millions of other Russian Jews would never have fled the pogroms of Eastern Europe for this great and opportunity-filled land of America.

Bernard Goldstein

CHAPTER ONE
THE NEW WORLD

On the first day of March 1881, Russian Tsar Alexander II was mortally wounded by a bomb attack sponsored by the anarchist group, The People's Will. The explosion did more than kill one man. It delivered the Russian Empire into the brutal and anti-Semitic hands of Alexander III and Nicholas II, led directly to the pogroms, and to one of the greatest mass migrations in history.

Alexander II had been a comparatively liberal and reform-minded ruler, abolishing serfdom and allowing Jews into the major cities. But his son and successor, Alexander III, believing liberalization had been a major factor in his father's assassination, hardened race and religion laws. Even though the Jews of Moscow and St. Petersburg had nothing to do with the anarchist movement, he threw them into the Pale of Settlement—the twenty five northernmost provinces of the Russian Empire, including Ukraine, Estonia, and Latvia.

Jewish residential, educational, and ownership rights were severely reduced. Encouraged by the authorities, vicious pogroms robbed Jews of their livelihoods, pillaged their homes and possessions, and even took their lives. Rumors were falsely spread that Jews were responsible for Alexander's assassination, and in 1903, the secret police published the forged *Protocols of the Elders of Zion*—minutes of a fictitious Zionist plot to take over the world.

In fear for their lives and drawn by the promise of freedom, 2.5 million Jews fled the Russian Empire for the United States between 1881 and 1914. They abandoned their homes, their work, and often their families, taking the newly emerging railroads to the ports of Western Europe, and then crowded passenger ships across the Atlantic. Few could speak or read English, and no assured jobs or income or government welfare awaited them at the other end. Such an undertaking was difficult, costly, and often traumatic. But for millions, including my wife's family, the Alters, and my own family, the Goldsteins, the alternative was far, far worse.

In 1900, Harry Alter left the Ukrainian city of Kiev for the United States. When he arrived, he was almost broke, but he spent his last pennies on a railroad ticket to

Morris Alter fled Russia for America in 1905. It was two years before he could afford to send for his family.

Looking west down Rock Island's 2nd Avenue in 1901.

Chicago. Chicago had nothing for him, however, so he bartered his overcoat with the railroad conductor for an extension, which took him to Rock Island, Illinois. Either Harry liked Rock Island or he had run out of coats, because he settled there, taking work as a scrap peddler. Three years later, he sent for his wife and children.

In 1905, his brother Morris also sailed for America and Rock Island. By 1907, he too had earned enough to send for his wife Ethel and their three children, Frank, Rose, and Besse. The children were very young for such a long journey: Frank was seven and Rose and Besse were four and three. From Kiev, they made the tough overland journey to the port of Rotterdam, Holland. On May 10, 1907, they boarded the SS *Statendam* and set sail for the New World. Nineteen days later, they docked at Ellis Island, off New York City. Then they set out for Illinois, where they reunited with Morris.

Morris had set up lodgings to welcome them at 23 7th Avenue in Rock Island, but they didn't stay there very long. By 1909, Morris and family were at 806 11th Street. In 1910, they moved to 612 7th Street. By 1915 they were living at 510 9th Street. But they never left the Rock Island-Davenport region. After all, aside from security, the towns offered the one thing for which Harry and Morris had journeyed halfway across the world: opportunity.

Immigrants landing at Ellis Island, ca 1910.

The region had once been a trading center of the American Fur Company and had seen some skirmishing during the War of 1812. In 1816, Fort Armstrong was established on Rock Island. In 1832, after the Indian Wars, linguist Antoine LeClaire helped negotiate peace with the Sac and Fox tribes, opening Iowa to settlers. In recognition, LeClaire was granted land opposite Rock Island. He later sold some land to Colonel Davenport, a supplier to the fort. The city of Davenport was founded there in 1836 and named in his honor.

In 1850, just 1,848 people lived in Davenport. In 1855, Davenport and Iowa City became the first towns in Iowa to have railroads, and one year later, Rock Island Lines built a railroad bridge over the Mississippi River, the first time a bridge had been built across a navigable waterway. When the steamboat *Effie Afton* struck and burned down the bridge, the St. Louis-based boat owners sued Rock Island Lines, claiming that the bridge constituted an impediment to traffic flow on the river. But the Rock Island Lines shrewdly retained Abraham Lincoln, then a rising Illinois lawyer,

Antoine LeClaire helped open Iowa to settlers after the Indian Wars.

to defend them, and he won the decision. The landmark case established the rights of railroads to cross rivers and enabled them to spread across North America.

Davenport and Rock Island grew quickly, as did the neighboring smaller towns of Bettendorf and Moline, which made up the urban district of the Quad Cities. A surge of German immigrants made German the most common language in Davenport. The town was packed with German shops and street signs, clubs and societies. Elsewhere, Belgians, Swedes, and Irish gathered in Rock Island and Moline, while many Mexicans settled in East Moline. By 1870, Davenport was a

George Davenport, for whom the city of Davenport was named.

key port for steamboats plying between St. Paul and New Orleans. Logs were rafted downstream from Minnesota, Wisconsin, northern Iowa, and Illinois. Cement companies quarried for limestone, and iron and steel companies were blessed with local raw materials. Farming machinery manufacturers like John Deere, J.I. Case, and

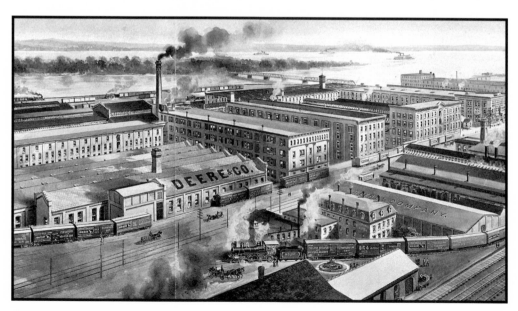

Factory buildings at Deere & Co.'s Moline Plow Works.

*Ronald Reagan, one-time sports
announcer on WOC radio.*

International Harvester sold many millions of dollars worth of equipment to midwestern farmers.

In 1888, Davenport introduced the second electric trolley system in the United States. By 1905, it was the second leading city in per capita wealth in the entire nation, and it had the most invested capital of all Iowa cities. It later boasted the second radio station in the United States, installed by B.J. Palmer, founder of one of the world's most prominent chiropractic schools. The station chose the call-letters WOC, and used the initials to advertise the "Wonders Of Chiropracty." (Incidentally, Benne Alter, Morris Alter's son, later worked at WHBF radio as a news announcer, where he competed for listeners against a WOC radio sports announcer by the name of Ronald Reagan.)

CHAPTER TWO
SCRAP

As Morris Alter, Harry Alter, and 2.5 million other East European Jews poured into the United States at the turn of the twentieth century, they were desperate for employment. Many were skilled, but there were few openings even for skilled Jews, particularly when they spoke no English. Often, they would spend their first months working at a Jewish-owned business, learning the language and a little about their new home. Then the more ambitious among them would set out on their own. Fortunately, one business required little capital or training and offered plenty of opportunity to those prepared to work hard: peddling scrap metal.

The industry was not new. For as long as there has been a metal industry, so there has been recycling of scrap. Genesis 4:22 refers to Tubal-Cain, seventh in descent from Adam, as an instructor of every artisan in brass and iron. He is widely credited with being the founder of the iron industry and the scrap metal industry, too.

Geoffrey Chaucer, father of English literature, was appointed clerk of the works at Westminster Palace at the Tower of London in 1389. One of his tasks was the collection and inventory of scrap metal. When the infamous Captain Kidd was captured in 1699, his ship's manifest recorded ten tons of scrap iron wheels in the hold. The first use of scrap metal in America was at Joseph Jenks' iron works at Saugus, Massachusetts. Jenks poured his first casting in 1642, just twenty-two years after the Pilgrims stepped ashore at Plymouth. Paul Revere used to advertise for scrap metals of all kinds in Boston newspapers, while George Washington ensured that old anchor chains were reused.

By the 1800s, iron was the heart of the American economy. Ships, railroads, guns, nails, screws, horseshoes, hoes, scythes, stoves, sewing machines, locks, wagon wheels, plows, and fences were all made of iron. Most iron was made by blast furnaces, melting iron ore, lime, and coke. But iron cracked easily and soon became scrap. The scrap was mostly useless, except when broken into small enough pieces to be melted in foundry cupolas along with pig iron from blast furnaces.

In 1856, Henry Bessemer invented an economical way to produce steel by blowing

*Henry Bessemer, inventor of the
Bessemer converter.*

cold air through molten pig iron, removing most of the carbon and so improving its strength and suppleness. Bessemer converters came to America in 1864. They soon made wrought iron obsolete and replaced cast iron in many applications. But like blast furnaces, Bessemer converters fed on raw materials, not scrap. All around America, old iron and steel were thrown in the back of sheds and barns and forgotten. A massive storehouse of scrap accumulated, and all that was needed was a way to use it.

In 1873, Andrew Carnegie negotiated an agreement to build America's first commercially successful open-hearth steel furnace, invented by German mechanic Charles William Siemens. Open-hearth furnaces, which fed half on scrap and half on pig iron from blast furnaces, soon became competitive with Bessemer converters. Gray iron foundries, large and small, also spread across the United States. These melted pig iron and scrap cast iron to make bathtubs, steam radiators, engine blocks, heavy machinery, and all other types of casting. Gray iron foundries and open-hearth furnaces opened up a whole new industry: the collection of iron and steel scrap for recycling.

Open-hearth furnaces in 1920.

Andrew Carnegie, founder of U.S. Steel, and at one time the world's richest man.

Charles Siemens, inventor of the open-hearth steel furnace.

Scrap dealing had one unusual aspect: it was an inverted industry. Instead of buying from a few suppliers and selling to many customers, scrap peddlers and dealers collected from many and delivered to few. Peddlers had to tour the countryside, collecting scrap metal, paper, rags, and rubber tires from houses, farms, and railroad stations. It was a hard and dirty job, and few people wanted it, so it was wide open to the influx of job-hungry Jews. As a result, a remarkable proportion of peddlers were Jewish immigrants. They soon became familiar figures, walking country lanes with backpacks or riding in a horse-drawn wagon filled with scrap. They then sold the scrap to yards, where it was sorted, processed, then delivered to mills and foundries.

II

When Harry Alter settled in Rock Island in 1900, he took work in a scrap yard that had been operating since 1898. Almost nothing is known about the very early days of that company, but when Morris Alter arrived in America in 1905, he joined his brother Harry in the business, and by 1908, the two men were joint proprietors of Davenport Iron & Metal Company at 522 West 2nd Street. In 1911, the company moved to 425 East 3rd Street.

Early scrap peddlers.

Early yards were not sophisticated, and most work was manual. All that a yard needed was half an acre of bare land, access to railroad tracks, and a big scale for weighing purchases. When peddlers brought wagonloads or truckloads of scrap to the yard, the scrap was weighed while still in the vehicle, then unloaded, inspected, and graded. The vehicle was weighed again after it was unloaded and the weight difference was then multiplied by price per ton to determine payment.

Yards bought all kinds of metal, from copper piping to zinc die cast. Aluminum pistons from car engines and lead from batteries were also salvaged and resold. But by far the largest volume was iron and steel, or "ferrous," scrap. Large iron castings were broken with sledgehammers. Railroad rail (a high-carbon steel) was nicked with a torch, then also broken with a sledgehammer. In winter, iron radiators were filled to the brim with water. When left overnight, the water would freeze, and the radiators would shatter. Heavy gauge steel was cut with alligator shears and acetylene torches into pieces no more than five feet long or eighteen inches wide. Number 1 grade was at least a quarter of an inch thick, while Number 2 was at least an eighth of an inch. Later, the maximum length of Number 2 grade heavy melting steel was reduced to three feet. Light gauge steel for many years was simply nonrecyclable and therefore discarded.

In 1913, at the age of thirteen, Morris Alter's son Frank started helping out at Davenport Iron & Metal, breaking iron in the yard or driving the horse and wagon around local communities to collect scrap. In 1916, at the age of sixteen, he left school to join his father and uncle full-time in their scrap metal and paper business. It couldn't have been easy for him, because Frank and his uncle didn't much like each other. After just a few months, Frank had had enough of Harry and left to start up his own business, Davenport Salvage Company, at 423 East 3rd Street, with Oscar Rotenburg, about whom little is known. The two men, with a horse and wagon purchased for $30, bought and sold scrap iron, metals, and rubber. They even had a listed telephone number: Davenport 7910. But in 1919, after three years on his own, Frank merged his company with that of his father and uncle. Frank and his father owned half of the new company, and Harry owned the other half. The terms of the agreement included an option enabling either of the two half-owners to set a price, at which the other could choose to sell or buy.

In 1920, Harry Alter exercised the option, shrewdly setting a price that he thought Morris and Frank couldn't afford. But Morris and Frank weren't to be so easily outmaneuvered. Convinced the price undervalued the business, they scraped and borrowed, determined to buy out Harry. Morris and Frank raised the sum and bought the business. They made it a general partnership, with Frank and his father each owning half, and renamed it Davenport Iron & Machinery. The acquisition left them not only deeply in debt but also woefully short of cash. In an effort to cut costs, they canceled their fire insurance, and almost immediately the warehouse holding their stock of scrap paper burned down. The loss almost bankrupted them, and from that time on, Morris and Frank specialized only in ferrous and nonferrous metals. Harry, despite a clause in the buy/sell agreement that prohibited him from setting up as a scrap dealer within fifty miles, established a rival business right next door. He called it Harry Alter & Sons, and ran it with his three sons, Louis, Franklin A., and Meyer. Over the following decades, people frequently—and often unfortunately—confused the two Alter companies.

Davenport Salvage Co.

Wholesale

SCRAP IRON - METALS - RUBBER

Second Hand Automobiles, Parts and Machinery

Phone: Dav. 7910

Office and Yards 425 E. Third Street   Davenport, Iowa

Frank Alter founded the Davenport Salvage Company in 1916.
Four years later, he merged with his father and uncle.

CHAPTER THREE
THE HOUSE THAT FRANK BUILT

Ralph Waldo Emerson once remarked that every great institution was the extended shadow of one man. If so, then Alter Company is the shadow of Frank R. Alter. Even if he didn't found today's company, he gave it its character, its ambition for growth, its taste for new technology, and its unbending integrity. Frank was about as fine a man as I have ever met, and his importance to the history of Alter Company merits a personal background.

Frank was born in December 1899, at the beginning of the twentieth century. Education was important to him. At school in America from the age of seven, he learned to speak, read, and write English. He had dreams of graduating from high school, then maybe studying medicine and becoming a doctor, but life had other plans for him. He was, after all, the eldest brother in what was now a family of eight children, and from the age of thirteen, he had to work at the scrap yard to help pay for house and food. That early experience taught him to respect money. He worked hard. He'd work at the yard before he left for school in the morning and again after he returned from school in the evening. At sixteen, his dreams of medicine finally faded, as he left school to join his father's scrap yard, then opened his own yard soon afterward.

Frank was born with white hair and eyebrows. One time, as a sixteen-year-old, he grew a mustache, and that was white, too, so he decided to darken it. He bought some dye from the local barber, and the barber instructed him to apply a moderate amount of the dye before he went to bed, and he'd wake up with such a richly colored mustache that he would be unable to recognize himself. The dye was clear, however, and Frank didn't believe a moderate amount was enough to do the job, so he splashed it on and rubbed it in vigorously. When he woke in the morning, he certainly couldn't recognize himself. Much of his hair, face, hands, and neck was blackened with dye, and he couldn't get it off, however hard he scrubbed. He had to go to work that day, still black as a lump of coal.

Frank Alter as a young man around 1920.

I I

The Davenport Iron & Machinery 3rd Street yard was very small, down by the railroad tracks. The company had no trucks at first, so Morris and Frank would go out on their horse and wagon to collect scrap iron and steel. One day, when Frank was out delivering scrap, his horse came to a dead stop and wouldn't move for begging or whipping. Frank had heard that the only way to move an exhausted horse was by lighting a fire under its backside, so he collected a good bundle of dry sticks, set them beneath the horse's rump and lit them. But the horse simply took a few weary paces forward and stopped again. Now the blazing fire was under the wagon, and Frank couldn't kick the fire out, or shift the horse again, before the wagon caught on fire and burned.

At first, the Davenport yard had little heavy equipment, but it did have the largest and heaviest sledgehammer that I had ever seen. Its head was so big that it needed two handles, so that Morris Alter and Jimmy Davidson could swing together and break iron castings. For his part, Frank used to cut cars apart with a hammer and chisel.

But while the yard started small, Frank had no intention of letting it stay that way. He may not have been as big or strong a man as his father, but his mind was tough as steel, and his ambition without limit.

Davenport, as part of the Quad Cities, was at the heart of the farm implement manufacturing industry and a center of iron foundries too—an ideal location in which to build a significant scrap yard. Even as a teenager, Frank visited major local buyers like French & Hecht and the Illinois steel mills at Peoria and Chicago in an effort to build relationships and sell scrap. One time, he visited John Deere, one of the farm

John Deere Model "D" tractor assembly line, 1924.

William Butterworth, John Deere's son-in-law and longtime leader of John Deere. His advice to the young Frank Alter helped shape Alter Company's character and integrity.

implement manufacturers based in Moline, Illinois, and called on William Butterworth, John Deere's son-in-law and chairman and CEO of the company, offering to supply cast iron scrap for the Deere foundries and to buy any steel or nonferrous scrap that Deere produced. The timing of Frank's visit was fortuitous. William Butterworth was evidently impressed with young Frank and awarded him some business.

Frank then asked Mr. Butterworth for advice on how to build a good company. At the time, some scrap metal dealers had bad reputations. Their trade was considered dirty and their ethics questionable. A few big dealers operated cartels, not bidding against each other for government and industrial scrap to ensure that prices remained low. Some small dealers fixed scales to benefit the yard, and peddlers occasionally loaded their carts with good scrap on top and rubbish below. "Son," said William Butterworth, with these practices in mind, "if you run a scrap iron business honestly, you will be a great success." Frank did, and he was.

III

As Davenport Iron & Machinery started buying and selling scrap to John Deere, so Frank began visiting Deere plants to advise them on the best ways of handling, ordering, and selling scrap. He became the leading scrap cast iron supplier to John Deere's foundries in Moline, Illinois, and to its tractor plant foundry in Waterloo, Iowa. His advice was invariably sound, and his relationship with John Deere grew ever closer.

Soon, John Deere plants were asking for consignments of scrap iron so large that Frank was unable to meet the demand from his own yard. He'd have to call up other yards in Iowa and surrounding states, buy scrap from them, then arrange to have it delivered to a John Deere foundry. That was the beginning of Frank's brokerage business. Brokerage helped Frank meet scrap cycles. In good times, he sold everybody's scrap; in slow times, he could always move his own scrap first. He quickly built up a good business, because purchasing agents wanted to buy from someone they could trust—and they knew they could trust Frank.

Scrap brokerage had some unusual aspects, as it still does today: for one thing, pricing works exactly the opposite of how most people would expect. The more scrap that customers want, the higher the price per ton they have to pay. That is partly because there is a finite quantity of available scrap at any particular time and place, and it shoots up in price the moment anyone starts bidding for it. It is also because identifying, negotiating, ordering, and delivering huge amounts of scrap is a whole lot of work.

The scrap market was therefore very volatile for brokers like Frank. Prices fluctuated day by day, season to season, year to year. Snowstorms and rail strikes could cause prices to rise as available scrap grew scarce, but often the markets moved without obvious cause. Such volatility made timing crucial and brokerage risky. A day's delay on a deal could turn a healthy profit into a big loss.

As a broker, Frank was responsible for the quality, quantity, and timeliness of the scrap deliveries he negotiated for his customers, so he was always vulnerable to unscrupulous dealers. But in practice, the scrap business was extraordinarily honorable. Deals worth tens of thousands of dollars were routinely made over the telephone, and with very rare exceptions, the deals were honored.

Logo of ISIS, forerunner of the Institute of Scrap Recycling Industries (ISRI).

Perhaps one of the best testimonies to Frank's fine reputation was his relationship with Keystone Steel in Peoria, Frank's first steel mill customer and a good customer to this day. Even so, scrap dealing had a poor reputation among some people. Frank, along with many other dealers, felt the need to improve the situation, and in 1928 many dealers banded together to form the Institute of Scrap Iron & Steel (ISIS), the forerunner of today's Institute of Scrap Recycling Industries (ISRI). The Institute helped the entire industry improve its image with the public and generate goodwill.

As one aspect of Frank's efforts to improve the popular image of scrap dealing, he always referred to himself as a scrap metal dealer, never as a junk man. One time, the city of Davenport insisted he get himself a junk dealer's license. It cost next to nothing, $3 or so, but Frank refused to buy. The city kept sending him letters, and he kept ignoring them. Eventually, city officials tried to cajole him. "Come on," they asked. "What's the matter with you?"

"I'm not in the junk business," he told them bluntly. "A junk is a Chinese boat. I've never bought one, and I've never sold one. I'm in the scrap metal business." Frank never did buy a junk dealer's license, but years later, when the city started calling it a scrap metal license, he bought one right away.

IV

By 1922, the yard was doing well, and Frank was eager to meet Yetta Gillman, the young woman his aunt had described to him with such enthusiasm. Yetta lived in De Soto, Missouri, about thirty miles south of St. Louis, so Frank drove down to meet her. She was not interested, however. She was eighteen, but it seemed like her family had been match-making for years. She'd met several young Jewish men and had liked none of them. She didn't see any reason why Frank should be different, so she messed

Yetta Gillman married Frank R. Alter in August 1923.

This is an early scrap handling crane. Alter Company was the
first scrap yard west of Chicago to install one.

up her hair, put on shabby old clothes, and waited grumpily for him to arrive.

Then Frank drove onto the Gillman's street and stepped out of his car. Yetta took one look at him from the apartment above their store and immediately changed into her very best clothes and fixed her hair. Frank and Yetta were married on August 19, 1923, in St. Louis, and later had two daughters, Anita and Irene (better known as Renee).

Progress at the yard continued through the 1920s, as Frank took over more and more control of the company. He showed himself to be a visionary, willing to try out new ideas and machinery. Although he'd raise Cain if money was wasted, he believed totally in the importance of heavy labor-saving machinery and any advantages technology could provide. The Davenport yard had the standard equipment by then,

including a scale for weighing
scrap deliveries and two alligator
shears for cutting steel. Then
Frank bought the first crane
used in any scrap yard west of
Chicago. Used mostly for loading
and unloading trucks and
railroad cars, the crane was also
equipped with a magnet that
could hoist a huge, heavy ball
high in the air, then drop it to
shatter large blocks of cast iron.
His friends and family warned
him he was crazy for spending
so much money on a crane that

*Depositors gather outside a Davenport bank in one of the
"panics" that followed the Wall Street Crash of 1929.*

they believed would inevitably bankrupt him. They were wrong.

What did nearly bankrupt him was the Wall Street Crash of October 29, 1929,
which sent the country and the world spiraling into the Great Depression. The
Depression was as bad for scrap as for every other industry. Frank survived, but not
without a scare or two. At the time, banks were very vulnerable to panics, as sudden
rumors prompted the populations of entire towns to demand their money at the same
time. It was a classic self-fulfilling prophecy: the panic made the fear come true. As a

result, people were reluctant to keep much cash
in their banks. One of those people, as Frank
discovered to his dismay, was Dan Hill of
Hill & Neiden of Lincoln, Nebraska, one of
Frank's longtime suppliers.

One day, Frank's own bank went bust, and
he lost all the money in his account, which was
more than he'd expected. But he thought no
more about the unexpected surplus in his
account (it was gone anyway) until a few
months later, when Dan Hill called. Dan told
Frank he still held one of his checks, written
before Frank's bank had gone bust, and now he
wanted it redeemed for cash. The sudden and
unexpected demand for cash put Frank close to
bankruptcy.

"You SOB," complained Frank, "why didn't
you cash that check when I sent it to you?"

"Because I trusted your credit more than I

*A Logemann Brothers baler
brochure around 1940.*

trusted the banks," answered Dan Hill. Frank honored the check, of course, but forever afterwards he was wary of going too deep into debt.

When business finally improved, Frank bought a Logemann baling machine for compressing light gauge steel scrap for open hearth furnaces. Before the baler arrived, Frank went around Iowa and Illinois collecting huge amounts of light gauge steel for virtually nothing. The mayor of Moline even called him and asked if he would get rid of the light gauge scrap from the city dumps. "Sure," said Frank, "bring it round." His yard filled with light gauge, and it took years to bale it all and ship it out. But like the crane, the baler proved a great investment, and other leading regional scrap yards soon purchased their own balers.

Frank also took his company into nonferrous metals. He built a furnace for melting aluminum into ingots, and also dealt in brass and copper. Many foundry customers liked copper as an additive, in the form of small pellets, or "shot," which was difficult to make. At first, copper dealers used to drop molten copper from a great height, so that it would spatter into droplets when it landed. That was expensive and awkward, so Frank—typically—invented his own rotary furnace for the task, pouring molten copper against a carbon electrode and spattering tiny copper pellets into a cold-water tank.

V

If the 1930s were bad for business, the outbreak of World War II made the 1940s an era of almost overwhelming demand. The war consumed materials at an unprecedented rate, and the king of materials was steel. Steel went into tanks, guns, ships, and planes. It fed munitions and armaments. The demand for steel after Pearl Harbor was extraordinary, and somehow scrap dealers had to meet it. In just one year, from 1942 to 1943, the number of scrap automobiles in U.S. auto wreckers and scrap yards plummeted from 15 million to 400,000!

Frank was offered a captaincy in the Navy, managing its recyclable scrap, but he turned it down because he could be more useful keeping the Davenport scrap yard working around the clock. His efforts at

Advertisement for the World War II
scrap recycling campaign.

Alter advertised for scrap during World War II, above.

The War Production Board coordinated America's World War II scrap collection effort, left.

Davenport were recognized when he was appointed to the War Production Board, working for the token salary of a dollar a year. The recommendation came from Charles Wiman, then CEO of John Deere, who was serving on the Board in Washington, D.C. Frank helped the Midwest contribute to the war effort, locating and supplying scrap metal for the steel mills and foundries in the region.

The Conservation and Salvage Division of the U.S. War Production Board coordinated a massive advertising and collection campaign, with 21,000 local salvage committees organizing more than 400,000 citizens. Cities, towns, and counties operated intensive scrap metal drives, and town squares filled with recyclable materials. Steel and iron were not the only materials being recycled. Rags and raincoats, used fat and old phonograph records had their use. Nylon stockings became parachute linings. Pennies lost color, as precious copper was diverted to war use. It was a time of innovation, imagination, and simply making do. You never knew exactly what material would be used for what purpose. I heard of one scrap dealer who bought a World War II submarine from the U.S. Navy and found that, because of the wartime copper shortage, the wiring was made of silver.

While the Great Depression and World War II were transforming the national economic landscape, Frank's company was changing too. In 1935, Davenport Iron & Machinery was renamed Alter Iron & Machinery Company. In 1938, the name was simplified to Alter Company. Then, on January 23, 1939, Morris Alter died. He left his estate to his wife, Ethel, and their eight children. With his share of the bequest and his own 50 percent holding in the company, Frank became majority shareholder. Over the next several years, he bought out his mother, brothers, and sisters, making himself the sole owner.

Irene (Renee) Alter in 1948.

In 1945, Frank admitted two of his brothers, Herman and Joseph C. Alter, into partnership. By December 1947, however, Herman and Joseph had become disillusioned with their prospects at Alter and sold their shares back to Frank. Herman and Joe then set up their own scrap company, called Joman Steel. At first, the brothers concentrated on new steel and pipe, but later they moved into scrap and became our competitors. They did okay for themselves, and even went after our accounts on occasion, but Frank instructed Chuck Smith and me never to go after theirs.

Herman and Joseph didn't leave Alter Company because it was doing poorly at the time. In fact, it was going through a sales and profits boom. The reason for their departure was that Frank's daughters had reached marriageable age, and Frank made no secret of the fact that he wanted to bring his sons-in-law into the family business and intended to hand over his share of the business to them. Anita, the elder daughter, married Arant Sherman in 1946, and he joined Alter in 1947. Then, to cap matters for Herman and Joseph, Frank's other daughter, Renee, was also soon to be married.

To me.

CHAPTER FOUR
THE GOLDSTEIN FAMILY

Like the Alters before them, many in my own family fled the pogroms of the Russian Empire for the safety of America. The family name was Tarasiuk, and they lived in the tiny village of Dobravilaitofska, one hundred miles north of Odessa in the north of Ukraine. My great uncle Jacob was first to leave. The eldest brother of my father's father, he emigrated to America before my grandfather was even born. Little is known of him, but he likely disembarked at Galveston, Texas, and then moved north up the Mississippi.

My grandparents (middle row) and parents (top row) with other members of the Borenstein and Goldstein families.

When last heard of, he had taken the name Goldstein and was living in the region of Davenport and Rock Island. Family legend says he chose Goldstein because he believed it to be a good American name! More likely, he was assigned it on arrival, because the immigration authorities couldn't understand his real name.

Chaika, Jacob, and Sonja Goldstein in the 1940s.

My family back in Ukraine didn't hear from him again and eventually believed he was dead. In line with the Jewish tradition of naming newborn children after deceased family members, my family gave my grandfather the name Jacob, in memory of his elder brother. In 1914, he too emigrated to America, adopted the Goldstein name, and went to Rock Island. He hoped to find news of his brother but had no success. Years later, however, his brother visited Rock Island for Passover. He had been living in

Irving, Rose, and Herman Goldstein in the 1940s.

Omaha. For the first and only time, the two brothers met. On learning that he had a younger brother named Jacob after him, the elder brother changed his name to Barney. He returned to Omaha and died a little later.

I was named Bernard after him.

My grandfather settled in Rock Island, peddling fish door to door to raise money so that he could send for his wife and children. But World War I broke out in Europe, and that was followed by the Russian Revolution. The Bolsheviks proved every bit as hostile to the Jews as the Tsars that preceded them, and they made emigration both

Market Square, Rock Island, in the 1920s.

Fannie and Morris (Fejga and Moishe) Goldstein.

difficult and dangerous. In 1922, Chaika, my grandmother, risked everything to sneak her five children (Udla, Ajzyk, Moishe, Chaim, and Sura in Russian, or Adele, Irving, Morris, Herman, and Sonia in English) over the Russian-Polish border in the dead of night. For the next several months, they waited at a Warsaw inn for my grandfather to send money and American papers. In that time, my twenty-one-year-old father, Moishe, fell in love with and married Fejga Borenstein, the innkeeper's daughter.

On October 24, 1923, the newly extended family boarded the SS *George Washington* at Bremen, on the northwest coast of Germany, and set off for the United States via Cherbourg, France, and Southampton, England. The 1,500 passengers were scheduled to disembark at Ellis Island, New York, but halfway across the Atlantic, the ship's captain heard that the annual quota for Russian immigrants was almost filled. As most of his passengers were Russian, he changed destination to Portland, Maine, a port he could reach more quickly. But when they docked on November 2, it was already too late. The quota was filled, and all Russian emigrants had to return to their port of embarkation.

It was a terrible moment for my family, fearing as they did that all those repatriated to Russia would face execution. But the Polish quota was not yet filled, and my Polish mother went to work on the immigration authorities at Portland, insisting that the whole family was from a small town just on the Polish side of the Russian border, which was why they could speak only Russian, not Polish! She must have been convincing, because the immigration authorities believed her. My family was in America at last.

In Illinois, they reunited with my grandfather, who was living at 6th Avenue and 9th Street in Rock Island, across the street from the synagogue. For their first few months, the family took jobs at a local clothing factory, leaving home before sunrise, and not finishing until after sunset. But they hadn't come halfway around the world to live like moles in perpetual darkness, so they quit their jobs, bought themselves an old truck, and began peddling the local countryside for scrap.

The family's unification in America brought great joy, and along with it, considerable gratitude toward the country that had offered them safe harbor and a new start. But our family's love of America had begun nearly a decade earlier. In 1914 or shortly thereafter, my grandfather wrote his family in Russia, recounting an experience he must have seen as vividly American, and laden with hope and promise: he was driving across the Mississippi River while at the same time a train roared on the tracks above him and boats plied the river below. What a wonderful, powerful country America is, he must have thought. My father inherited that spirit. He frequently urged his children to visit other countries so that they might better appreciate what a great country America is.

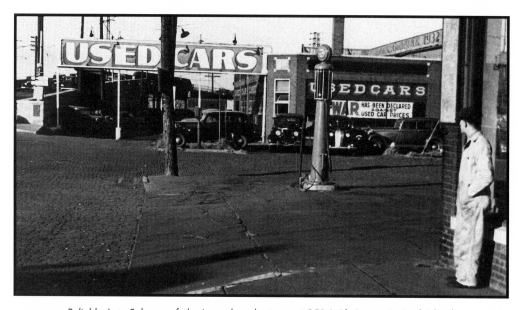

Reliable Auto Sales, my father's used car business at 2514 4th Avenue in Rock Island.

I I

One time, my father bought an old car intending to break it up and sell it for scrap, but he sold it as a used car instead, and in so doing established himself as the first used car dealer in Rock Island. He set up Reliable Auto Sales at 2514 4th Avenue, and later brought his brothers into the business. Herman later became a Chrysler dealer in Moline, Illinois, while Irving, after serving as a soldier in World War II, sold Hudson and Studebaker autos and opened the Stardust Hotel in Moline.

The used car business was still young when my father started, and finance companies wouldn't loan money for car buyers unless the dealer was prepared to guarantee the loan. My father therefore arranged credit for his customers with finance companies. That was fine until the Great Depression. Then his customers stopped making their payments, and the finance companies came after my father and his guarantees. Money became very tight. By 1932, our family finances were so bad that my mother took my elder brother Sidney and me back to Warsaw, where we stayed in our grandfather's inn for a year until business improved and we returned to the United States.

That was the first and only time I met my mother's parents. A few years later, they were caught up in the horror of the Holocaust. Luckily, my mother's two brothers survived the war. In 1937, my uncle Joe came to America. My uncle Moishe Borenstein was serving in the Polish army at the time of Hitler's invasion of Poland in 1939. Realizing he was in grave danger, my grandparents took him to the Lithuanian border and bought him a ticket on the Trans-Siberian Railway. They returned to Warsaw themselves and were never heard from again.

Moishe took the railway across the Soviet Union to China. In December 1941,

Moishe Borenstein and Morris Goldstein.

Japanese troops in Shanghai.

he reached the Japanese-occupied city of Shanghai; my parents had bought him passage on a ship from Shanghai to the United States. Two weeks before his ship was scheduled to sail, however, Japan attacked Pearl Harbor, and the whole world was at war. Moishe was stranded. For four years, he lived on his wits and the few Red Cross packages that actually reached him. It was not until after the war that he finally left Shanghai for America.

Many years later, in the fall of 1994 and long after Moishe had passed away, I was invited by Salomon Brothers to join a panel in Jerusalem discussing the economic impact of casinos. It was the first regional economic conference after the peace talks, and was sponsored by the Tourism Department of Israel, which hoped that casinos might boost the Israeli economy through tourism. The conference center was packed with media, but not for us. In the next room, Shimon Peres was leading a discussion on the economics of peace. Understandably, he got more of the media spotlight than I did.

On our last night, Salomon Brothers threw a party for us at the King David Hotel, and I sat next to a young New York lawyer named Rosen. I mentioned to him that I had recently been in Shanghai, visiting the area where the Jews had lived through World War II, hoping to learn a little about my uncle's experience. Rosen looked at me in surprise and asked my uncle's name. Moishe had passed away some time before, and for some reason I was reluctant to answer. But Rosen became insistent, so I told him my uncle was Moishe Borenstein.

"*I knew it,*" he exclaimed.

"Knew what?"

His father, he told me, had also been stranded in Shanghai through the war. His best friend through the nightmare had been Moishe Borenstein, but somehow they had lost touch after the war. Rosen's father had always talked fondly of Moishe and had wondered what had happened to him. Sadly, he too had recently passed away. "The best friends are together again," he said.

Moishe, Joe, and my mother were the only members of my mother's family to survive the war. I remember a postcard we received in 1940, with swastikas on the corners, informing my mother that her father had passed away. After that, she received no news at all of her sister, or her sister's children, or any other members of her family. She was sick with worry throughout the war, and afterwards she drove herself frantic contacting agencies, trying desperately to trace any family members that might somehow have survived the gas chambers of the Holocaust.

She had lost them all.

III

I was born on February 5, 1929, just months before the Wall Street Crash. I don't remember much about the bad times of the Great Depression or even the war, but I do remember many good things about my childhood in the Quad Cities. We lived at 909 12th Avenue, Rock Island, right next door to our lifelong friends, the Weindruchs. Our houses were so close together, Frank Weindruch used to complain he couldn't sleep because of my father's snoring.

I remember riding down to the Mississippi River on my bicycle, taking the Quinlan Ferry to Davenport, and on two occasions taking the excursion boats to Muscatine and back. My lifelong love for the river was born then, an endearment that influenced Alter's entry into the barge line business and later into riverboat gaming.

The W.J. Quinlan Ferry on the Mississippi River during the 1940s.

Sidney Goldstone, my elder brother, practiced medicine in Gary, Indiana.

Growing up, two of my closest friends were Sonny Kavensky and Herb Spector. By some coincidence, all three of us went on to become attorneys, although they practiced law and I didn't.

I was the middle of three sons. Sidney was my senior by four and a half years. We got on like most brothers, fighting a lot but standing up for each other too. Sidney studied medicine and became a general practitioner, and was then invited to join his cousins (Barney's children) Joe and Adolf Goldstone in their practice in Gary, Indiana. They refused to call their practice Goldstone, Goldstone, and Goldstein, so Sidney changed his last name to Goldstone. Despite warning me against smoking and never smoking in my presence, he smoked all his life and died from lung cancer in 1988.

My younger brother, Arthur, also became a doctor and joined the same practice. He too changed his name to Goldstone, then married and started a wonderful family. He became a pilot and owned a half interest in a twin-engine Comanche. On March 24, 1974, after a skiing holiday, Arthur flew his wife Lillian and their three children, Gerald, Debra, and Mark, out of Aspen Airport in Colorado. Shortly after takeoff, Arthur failed to answer radio calls and was not heard from again. The Colorado Civil

Arthur Goldstone, my younger brother, also practiced medicine in Gary, Indiana. He died tragically with his family when his airplane crashed outside Aspen, Colorado.

Air Patrol and the U.S. Air Force began an intensive two-week search of a 5,000-square-mile area. Initial aerial photographs showed no trace of plane wreckage. Because the plane was white, with red and black markings, there was little hope that it would show up against the snow, so they tried infrared photography as well, but that failed too.

In desperation, my brother Sidney and I offered a $50,000 reward, but still the plane was not found. Hope faded into acceptance of the tragic truth, and eventually the official search was called off. In gratitude for the efforts of the search and rescue teams, Sidney and I put money toward a fund to provide equipment for civilian search units. Three months later, a newly licensed pilot discovered Arthur's plane. It had crashed into a peak eight miles from Aspen Airport. Just two hundred feet higher, and it would have cleared the mountain.

IV

Since our father was in the car business, he used to bring home a different car every week. As a result, I learned to drive at a young age. When I was just eleven years old, I'd come home from school for my lunch and spend the hour driving the latest car around the block. But then World War II badly disrupted the auto business as Detroit geared for military production, and my father had to close up. For a while he took work on the night shift in an East Moline stamping plant to pay for Sidney's medical studies.

Then, toward the end of the war, the army started selling off surplus trucks. With Vern Johnson, and later his brother Norman, my father borrowed money from V.O. Figge at the Davenport Bank & Trust and bought a consignment of trucks from Camp Crook, near Omaha, Nebraska. The trucks were mostly falling apart, except they had brand-new tires, which were very scarce at the time. The partners made enough money from selling the tires to cover their costs, so that the rest of the trucks were profit. Many were sold to the contractor who was building a new plant in Davenport for Alcoa. Others were sold to local farmers for spreading lime.

My father bought surplus trucks from all over the country. One time, in 1944, he heard that the army was selling new Studebaker 6x6 trucks still in crates in Port Huineme, California. He sent me in a station wagon with four truck drivers to drive them back to Bettendorf, Iowa. I was supposed to drive the station wagon on the return journey, going ahead of the convoy, arranging rooms and supplies and making sure everything went smoothly. One of the drivers decided he wanted that job, however, and swapped with me. Now I had to drive an army truck, towing another truck, back to Bettendorf. I was just fifteen years old.

It was all going fine until we came to the Rocky Mountains. We drove through them at night, following each other's headlights around the narrow curves. Then we started coming down, and I found out how difficult it could be to drive one truck with a second towed truck racing along immediately behind it. The only way I could control it was to accelerate down the mountain, pumping my horn to warn other drivers I was coming. One time, I came up fast behind a house that was being moved on the highway, and I honked it off the road with only a second to spare, then missed it by a coat of paint. I finally ran out of luck in Kansas, where my truck jack-knifed, buckling the tow bar. We weren't licensed to drive through Kansas, and I was too young to be licensed at all, so the other drivers shrewdly fled for the state line, leaving me to deal with the situation.

Inevitably, a police officer came along. I had borrowed my brother Sidney's driver's license, but even that didn't qualify me to drive anything as heavy as those trucks. Thankfully, I was big for fifteen, and the officer didn't question my age or the license. Instead, he asked me why I had no authorization to pass through Kansas. "They're Army trucks," I told him. "Army vehicles are exempt." Not only did he believe me, by some miracle, but he also helped me fix the towbar.

In 1952, my father changed careers again and became a real estate developer, building low-cost waterfront homes in Hollywood, Florida. He was very good at it, too, building hundreds of homes in several different sites. When developing one site, he struck a layer of rock. Unabashed, he promptly turned the site into a quarry. He was a true entrepreneur, making the best out of every situation he found himself in, and he taught me a tremendous amount about business. He also infected me with his love of dealing. When asked "how's business?" he'd reply either "on the rocks" or "going deeper in the hole."

My brother Sidney told me about a program at the University of Illinois at Champagne that allowed people to start college at sixteen. I took the tests, qualified for the liberal arts program, then continued on to law school. I met Irene Alter while we were still both teenagers. I knew nothing of her family then, except for a faint memory of cleaning up our garage at the used car lot and taking a truckload of scrap to the Alter yard in Davenport. Irene and I were married in 1949, while I was still

My father developed homes in Hollywood, Florida.

With Renee on our wedding day in 1949.

studying law. We honeymooned on the Gulf Coast and spent half a night in Biloxi, Mississippi, a town that would prove significant later in my life.

Frank, my new father-in-law, invited me to make a career with him at Alter after I finished law school. I asked for a year to make up my mind, and spent two or three days a week in the scrap yard, commuting to law school in Iowa City on the remaining days to get enough hours to graduate. In 1951, I passed the Iowa bar exam and became a lawyer. I couldn't put off the decision any longer. It was time to pick between courtroom scraps and scrap metal. In the end it was not that difficult. I gave up law and joined Alter full-time, and full of enthusiasm.

CHAPTER FIVE
ALTER: 1950–1960

In 1950, Alter employed nearly one hundred people at its single property, a twenty-six acre scrap yard at 1701 Rockingham Road on Davenport's west side. Two brick buildings accommodated 27,800 square feet of space. A 1950 *Dun & Bradstreet* analytical report noted that Alter wholesaled a complete line of scrap iron and steel and nonferrous metal, as well as new iron and steel sheets, plates, bars, and beams; it also handled a line of new and used machinery, pipes, factory supplies, and wiping cloths. Alter had extensive equipment for a scrap yard of the time, and manufactured its own aluminum

The Alter yard at 1701 Rockingham Road, Davenport.

ingots and copper shot. Operations were financed from working capital, supplier comment was good, and the yard did seven figures worth of annual profitable business.

We had a good crew of people at the Davenport yard. They worked hard, had a positive attitude, and kept the place neat. We were very busy, I remember. The Korean War was just starting and we were working around the clock, supplying scrap to steel mills and foundries for guns, tanks, shells, and other munitions. Scrap was in frantic demand, but wartime price controls limited profit. While some other dealers ignored those restrictions, Frank insisted we deal legally. For a time, that caused us severe problems, but fortunately my legal training proved its worth as we found a way to bring scrap through the Davenport yard to add value and ensure that the higher charges were appropriate.

Watching Frank work was an education. He had an incredible brain for detail, knowing to the penny how much everything in the yard had cost. He did some of everything: brokering deals on the phone, calling on accounts, getting out and about in the yard, talking to the crews. Under his leadership, the yard had grown big, but he had never really learned to delegate, so his workload stretched him to the limit. He typically arrived before six in the morning, and worked till late in the evening, six or seven days a week. He was a man of habit. Willie Cooper, one of our long-serving employees, remarked that you could set your clocks by the times he walked through the scrap yard, twice a day, every day. He knew everyone by name, and he'd always find time to talk to them.

*The Logemann Press at the Rockingham Road
scrap yard in 1940.*

Frank Alter continued to build Alter Company's reputation and business through the 1940s and 1950s.

Weighing-in at the Alter yard scales.

Frank wanted to do everything himself, but it wasn't possible. I knew early on that if the business was to grow, Frank had to share his responsibilities. When I first started working for him, he'd take me out into the yard and teach me how to weigh the incoming trucks and inspect railroad cars filled with scrap. That could be an experience. Scrap was, and still is, shipped in open-top gondola cars with four-inch-wide ledges around the rim. The ledges were usually beaten up from having been hit with scrap or heavy magnets, but Frank would climb up and walk nonchalantly around them, as though they were four-lane highways. I tried to imitate him, but being big and clumsy, I was far too anxious about which way to fall if I lost my balance and could never concentrate. Eventually I took the coward's way out, picking my way across the load itself or just using the gondola's ladders.

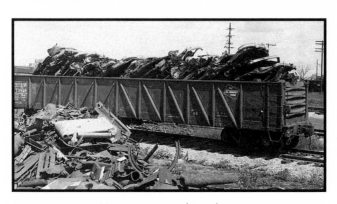

Moving scrap metal in railcars.

Frank made me feel very welcome—but then he welcomed anyone who was prepared to work hard. He knew how to make people feel part of the Alter family. As far as he was concerned, everybody at Alter was important, but nobody—himself included—was exceptionally important. When Alter earned its first check for half a million dollars, for instance, Frank made copies of the check and distributed them to everyone at the yard. That was the way he thought: Alter's success was everyone's to share.

We had no unions at the time, no official health plan, and no pension plan, but that didn't mean Frank neglected his people. He paid competitive salaries and bonuses, and when employees needed help with medical bills for themselves or their families, Frank would pay them out of his own after-tax earnings. He personally financed pensions for long-time employees. Sometimes, on Saturday mornings, Frank would even go down to the jailhouse to bail out Alter employees who'd had too much to drink the night before.

The system (or lack of it) was very generous but expensive. I persuaded Frank to bring in comprehensive company health and pension plans so that we could finance them with pre-tax income. We also added a company-wide profit-sharing plan, which helped us attract and keep some good young managers like Chuck Smith, who

Chuck Smith joined Alter Company in 1953 and quickly became one of my closest friends.

Dee Lesher, our telephone operator for better than thirty years.

joined us as a buyer and seller of scrap in 1953. Chuck, then a twenty-eight-year-old native of Bettendorf, Iowa, and graduate of Davenport's St. Ambrose College, soon became one of my greatest friends and one of Alter's finest people. When Dee Lesher joined Alter as a switchboard operator in 1964, she spent her first four hectic days asking for help from the person with the friendliest and kindest voice. That turned out to be Chuck Smith, who was by then vice president, chief buyer, and head of all scrap merchandising. Dee also remembers how Frank Alter came out to meet her late on her first day, shaking her hand warmly and apologizing for not welcoming her earlier. Coming from a huge public utility company, that courtesy from the company president enchanted her.

Dee has been with Alter for over thirty years now, and no one has ever had a better phone operator. She has an incredible ear for voices, and she's been a pleasure for our customers to deal with and a tremendous asset to the company. One time, some of our office staff were considering forming a union until Dee started talking to them. She told them about Frank and me, the history of the company, and the way we all worked together as a family. She told them the truth—that joining a union wouldn't benefit them, because Frank already looked after his people as well as his company could afford. Soon she'd reduced them all to tears. That was the last time our office workers ever considered a union.

I wish Dee had talked to our truck drivers too. Quad Cities' industry had been strongly unionized even before World War II, and many workers at John Deere, International Harvester, and J.I. Case belonged to the UAW, but Alter had always been non-union. We'd built up quite a fleet of trucks by this time, however. After all, freight costs were an integral part of the ferrous scrap business, comprising about a quarter of the total price. In fact, freight was so important that scrap dealers pioneered containerization long before the "container revolution" took place. As early as 1951, we had open-top containers at our major customers, dropped off and picked up by our own specially equipped trucks. Later, we introduced a double container so that one truck could haul two different scrap loads at the same time, cutting costs and enabling collection from cities as distant as Des Moines, 175 miles away.

Now, all of a sudden, we learned that our truckers wanted to join the Teamsters Union. To Frank, who considered all employees part of his family, the vote to join the union was a real disappointment, as if he couldn't be expected to look after those who worked for him. Treating his people fairly and well meant a great deal to Frank, and he was always available to his employees. It hurt him deeply that the truckers thought they needed a union representative to speak for them, and Frank never enjoyed work in the same way afterwards.

That said, the Teamsters proved sensible and businesslike. They wouldn't deliberately bankrupt a business, as some unions would. A few years later, when we were interested in buying a barge terminal in Rock Island, we had to deal with the Teamsters again. The business had been run into the ground, and there was little hope for it. Part of the problem was that the Teamsters had gotten the wages up to nearly double the average rates until the company wasn't competitive any more. We told the Teamsters that the only way we'd take over the terminal was with standard Alter contracts. Aware that it would close altogether if they refused, they accepted, and they deserve credit for that. Not every union acted so wisely. In one notorious instance, a union drove a small Moline company into bankruptcy, just to prove their point.

I I

Although Frank was both generous and loyal to his people, he could be just as tough as he needed to be. A peddler from Muscatine regularly used to sell scrap to our Davenport yard. He'd weigh in loaded, go into the yard, take off his tailgate, unload his scrap, weigh empty, get his cash, then go back and pick up his tailgate. That way, the weight of the tailgate was factored into his payment for scrap, and over time, he was cheating us out of hundreds of dollars.

One day, an Alter employee spotted him hiding his tailgate and told Frank. Next time the peddler came in, he went into his usual routine: he weighed in, took off his tailgate, unloaded his scrap, weighed empty, then collected his check. But when he went back to get his tailgate this time, it was gone. He stormed into the office shouting blue murder, protesting that someone had stolen his tailgate, demanding to see Frank.

Frank came out, cool as a cucumber. "What are you talking about?" he asked. "It's my tailgate. I must have bought it off you a hundred times." Frank didn't give it back, either, and the peddler went off cursing and vowing he'd never sell us another thing. He was as good as his word too, for at least a week.

Another time, we bought scrap for later delivery from a scrap dealer, and the dealer failed to ship because the market price of scrap went up in the interim. That meant that we had to make good on the delivery from our own yard, which cost us plenty.

We didn't trade with that dealer for a long, long time, but years later, when he thought we'd forgotten all about the incident, we made another purchase from him, paying him $2 more a ton than he could get elsewhere. After he'd delivered, we simply deducted what he owed us from his payment. It was funny to listen to him as he cussed me out, because we were right and he knew it, and there was not a thing in the world he could do about it. After that, interestingly, he became one of our regular suppliers.

Such episodes were very unusual, but they did happen. One steel mill once rejected a carload of scrap we had brokered, complaining that it was contaminated with lead and aluminum and other nonferrous materials. I called the yard from which we had bought the load and notified them that it was contaminated and had been rejected.

"But that's impossible," they protested. "That load was fine. They can't have checked it."

"How can you be so sure?" I asked.

"Because the railroad track is being repaired," they answered. "The railroad hasn't even pulled that car yet. It's still here."

Despite these rare episodes, I soon learned that scrap was a very honorable trade. In fact, it was remarkable how few bad guys there were. In brokerage, particularly, a man's word was his bond and a thing of great pride. Alter had a very good broker at the time named Sam Edelman. Sam was Frank's right-hand man and my first mentor. He stayed a long time at Alter, until Arant named his dog Sam after him. Sam took it personally and left us for a job in Milwaukee.

One of my first assignments was to sell an entire airstrip! Frank and Arant had bought it from the military in 1950, mistakenly thinking they could sell it to Howard Hughes. As a result, we had six thousand tons of 2' x 20' Irving Grid steel landing mats on our hands. They were very costly to cut up for scrap, so we needed to be creative. I tried to sell them back to Pentagon officials, who were buying new, similar landing mats for the Korean War. They needed the mats but didn't dare buy them in case the media found

Sam Edelman, Frank's right-hand man and my first mentor at Alter Company.

out and ridiculed them for buying back at a premium the mats they had just sold for scrap!

Then I had an inspiration—or so I thought. We'd sell the strips to farmers as cattle guards, to stop cows from getting out of the pasture. We advertised the strips in agricultural newspapers, priced cheap, and sold them all over the Midwest, in Iowa, Wisconsin, and Indiana. For a while, I was the hero of the company. Three months later, the first phone calls came in, complaining that the cattle had learned how to cross our cattle guard. One lady said that even her chickens were getting out.

As more and more calls came in, from angrier and angrier farmers wanting a refund, I went to Frank and asked what to do. Without hesitation, he told me to give the money back.

My first major assignment was to find a way to sell these landing mats.

It cost us plenty, and we still had the mats on our hands, but at least we kept our reputation, and that was the most important thing. We sold some mats to Northwestern Steel & Wire Company for walkways in a new plant, and cut up others for scrap. Later, we had the idea of selling them as ramps to get boats into the water. They proved perfect for that, and when the word got out, we were deluged with requests, but by that time we had only two hundred tons left.

Working in brokerage gave me the chance to talk to other dealers and learn about their businesses. That taught me plenty about the scrap industry as a whole. It didn't take me long to see that we were in a period of great transition, for three main reasons. First, most yards were then still family owned, but the people who had built them up were getting on in years. Their children, looking instead toward law, medicine, and the other professions, were often not interested in carrying on the family business.

Second, some powerful new equipment was coming onto the market, and the old-style scale-and-sledgehammer yards couldn't compete with those investing in new hydraulic shears, presses, and trucks. But that new machinery was very expensive and couldn't be financed without bank loans. Many dealers who'd struggled through the Depression couldn't bear the thought of taking on such huge debts.

Third, the environmental movement was just beginning to threaten the scrap business with all kinds of clean-up costs as well as an enormous increase

A metal shear, one of the new pieces of equipment that enabled a new approach to the scrap metal business in the 1950s and 1960s.

in the administrative burden. To most dealers, paperwork was as welcome as a bad case of gastric flu. For all these reasons, many dealers put their yards up for sale or simply closed them. But not Alter. We wanted to grow.

III

In 1956, the city of Davenport decided to put a four-lane highway straight through our yard at 1701 Rockingham Road. That would have made it tough to do business, so we decided to relocate. We found the site on which Davenport Besler had been manufacturing steam locomotives for many years. It was ideal for us, with several large old buildings and plenty of railroad track. At 46 acres, it was 20 acres bigger than our previous site. That gave us the opportunity to design a whole new style and layout, where we could greatly increase our volume without increasing our costs. I persuaded Fritz Zettle, a local engineer, to join us, and together we laid out our new yard. Everything was designed to operate at the lowest cost per ton, from weighing stations to the design of our overhead cranes, from the layout of machines to car-switching facilities.

Alter Company acquired the Davenport Besler site in 1956.

Expansion Edition Times - Democrat Saturday, Feb. 15, 1958

Alter Firm Continues Spectacular Growth

A 213 per cent increase in sales since 1954 has moved the Alter Co. into position as a major factor in the steel scrap business and the largest producer of secondary nickel alloys in the world.

To meet this spectacular growth and also prepare for further expansion, the Alter Co. bought, in 1956, the 42 acre tract once occupied by the Davenport Besle. Corp. at 2333 Rockingham Road.

Moving from its old location, the company has increased its physical plant many times over at the new 42 acre site.

There are 218,000 square feet of space in the buildings at the new site.

During the past year the Alter Co. has spent major sums of money completely renovating the area to suit its own specialized needs.

This work included the installation of such major items as cranes, furnaces, electrical systems, and railroad track.

A major improvement in the expansion of the Alter Co.'s iron and steel scrap business was the purchase and installation of a huge press which is used to bale the material before shipping.

dent, and Bernard Goldstein, secretary-treasurer.

The technological requirements of industry and the military have become more complicated every year. Their needs have required an ever expanding number of alloys of high quality.

Anticipating these demands, Alloy Metal Products Inc., was formed in 1950 under the direction of Arant H. Sherman.

The company has applied scientific skills to the reclamation of nickel alloy scrap and its manufacture into ingot and pig metal.

In a short span of seven years this company has become the world's largest producer of these secondary nickel alloys.

Nickel alloys are used in such things as missiles, jet engines, and other machinery that requires a heat resistant metal, as well as, such consumer products as stainless steel kitchens and automobile trim.

Officers in Alloy Metal Prod-

Pictured above is an aerial view of the new 42-acre Alter Co. plant. The area was formerly occupied by the Davenport Besler Co. Over five miles of railroad track serve the sprawling plant. The numbers in the picture above correspond to the following plant operations: (1) Metallurgical laboratory, (2) melt shop, (3) hydraulic baling press, (4) maintenance shop, (5) warehouse and shipping, (6) processing building, (7) truck loading dock, (8) office building.

Even the local newspapers were impressed by our achievements in the 1950s.

The next challenge was to take advantage of our new size and efficiency by increasing our intake of scrap. By now, a substantial proportion of our scrap came from old cars. We already took much of the car scrap from the auto wrecker yards around the Quad Cities, however, and it was not economical at the time to truck in car bodies from very far afield, because we could fit only six unflattened cars on a flatbed trailer. If we could haul twenty cars, I thought, then we could make longer hauls pay off.

I had an idea. Al Sharp and Jon Kneen of Ottumwa, Iowa, were working with us at the time designing and building truck trailers. I approached them to design a concept I had for a portable flattener that could crush a car in such a way that it could still be stacked on a flatbed and hauled on the highway. They did it. The machine I helped design could squash car bodies into four-inch metal pancakes, which meant we could crush cars at auto wrecker yards and pile twenty tons of payload onto a flatbed truck trailer. Suddenly, we could afford to buy bodies from as far away as 150 miles if we had something to haul to that site. By hauling coal, for instance, from the river into the interior of Iowa and coming back with flattened auto bodies, we could have all the incoming volume we needed. This invention proved to be a major advance in the scrap business, and soon became an industry standard.

Now, so that we could handle all the extra volume, we had to improve our processing. We began

This portable auto flattener enabled us to pile twenty tons of car bodies onto a flatbed truck.

looking at state-of-the-art equipment. We bought an 8,000-pound electromagnet, the largest then being manufactured. In 1957, I also heard about a huge hydraulic baling machine made by Harris of Cordele, Georgia, which could bale a whole car at a time. It cost a staggering $2 million, but I knew it would be worth every penny if it

A flatbed truck picks up crushed cars from an auto wrecker's yard.

meant we no longer had to cut cars into quarters before feeding them to the baler. There was a prototype Harris machine in Nate Rose's Chicago yard, but Nate was not about to show it to his competitors. I went up to Chicago anyway and sneaked a peek over the fence from the plant next door. I liked what I saw. So we purchased a Harris 3000 and eventually installed it in the yard.

Not long after, an unfortunate incident occurred in that building. It was about January 1958 and very cold. As a result, the building's sprinkler system froze, breaking the pipes and flooding the basement. The worst part was that in the basement we had stored all of the old "Golden Girl" calendars, dating back many years. In the early 1940s, Alter Company had begun putting out calendars featuring a picture of a "golden girl"—a girl in a golden bathing suit. Those calendars had become a tradition, which continues to this day. To our considerable dismay, all the calendars before 1957 were ruined by the flooding.

Our new equipment massively increased our turnover. Our next challenge was to increase our sales. In 1957, our major customers were all local foundries, or the steel mills in Chicago, Peoria, and Sterling, Illinois, to which we could rail our scrap for no more than $5 per gross ton. These customers knew we had a limited distribution range, and therefore they could always underbid the market, putting pressure on our margins. If we truly wanted to grow, we somehow needed to expand our sales range to include St. Louis, Pittsburgh, and other key markets, without paying more for freight.

And that meant a whole new approach.

CHAPTER SIX
TRANSPORT

"It is hereby declared," reads Section 500 of the 1920 Transportation Act, "to be the policy of Congress to promote, encourage and develop water transportation, service and facilities in connection with the commerce of the United States, and to foster and preserve in full vigor both rail and water transportation."

The Mississippi River runs like a backbone down the middle of America's inland waterways system. For navigation purposes, it is divided in two sections: the Lower Mississippi, which extends from the Gulf Coast to Cairo, Illinois (pronounced Kay-row), and which is navigable by big boats; and the Upper Mississippi, which stretches from Cairo up to Minneapolis, Minnesota.

Towboat and barges on the Mississippi River in 1923.

Keokuk lock, drydock, and boat yard in 1938.

In 1931, the Rock Island electorate voted 6,450 to 2,077 in favor of building a local river terminal, at a cost of $380,000. By 1938, twenty-six locks and dams had been built between Minneapolis and Alton, Illinois. The system assured boats a minimum nine-foot-deep channel of navigable water on the Upper Mississippi, at least when it was not frozen. In 1935, the *Davenport Democrat* prophesied that a "huge tonnage" would make the Quad Cities a "great industrial site." The Federal Barge Line, helped by federal government subsidies, proved the prediction correct, and tonnage raced past the one million mark. In 1953, Federal Barge was sold to the St. Louis Ship Company, and the industry effectively opened up to private enterprise.

The Upper Mississippi was coming into its own.

As a young boy, I'd watched from the banks of the river as the towboats pushed barges of coal, steel, grain, sand, stone, and other materials up and down the river. I didn't realize it then, but the Mississippi River's junctions with the Ohio, Missouri, and Illinois Rivers, as well as other navigable waterways, created a network that connected the Quad Cities with many key industrial areas, including St. Paul, St. Louis, New Orleans, Pittsburgh, Kansas City, Cincinnati, Chicago, and even Brownsville, Texas, on the Mexican border.

By 1956, I was driving almost every day along the Mississippi River, frequently shuttling between Davenport and Rock Island, or Bettendorf and Moline. I couldn't help but notice that barge traffic was increasing. The idea just came to me one day that maybe it would be viable to deliver scrap metal by barge. I called an official of Blaske Barge Line, based in St. Louis, who told me they'd moved a few loads of scrap iron out of St. Paul, Minnesota. When I asked for rates from Davenport to Alton and St. Louis, they quoted me about $2.50 per gross ton. That was exciting news. The St. Louis area had two mills, Laclede Steel and Granite City Steel. We'd never sold to these mills before because freight costs by rail had always been prohibitive. Now at $2.50 a gross ton, whole new markets had suddenly opened up to us.

In those days, Frank, Arant, Sam, Chuck, and I used to lunch together at the Blackhawk Hotel. It was a terrific way of keeping in touch with what was going on and a good forum for debating new ideas. One lunch, I shared my idea with Frank and the others, and they encouraged me to proceed.

It wasn't easy. We had some serious headaches to deal with. For one thing, each barge carried the same volume as twenty railroad cars or seventy-five trucks—a huge amount of scrap. For another, we couldn't just sail barges into our yard for loading and unloading. We needed a waterfront property. I soon found a suitable property on the Davenport seawall, four miles from our yard. It already had railroad tracks and needed only a crane for loading and unloading. But when I applied to the Levee Commission of the city of Davenport for a license, they told me they preferred that barge loading be done from Rock Island. That was no use to me, though, because the cost to get there was too high, so I had Frank call Walter Priester, head of the Levee Commission, and we got a temporary, renewable, one-year lease. We still have it.

In 1957, we trucked our first load of scrap down to the Davenport seawall, loaded it by crane onto a Blaske barge, then shipped it to Laclede Steel at Alton, Illinois, just north of St. Louis. It was the first time anyone in the Quad Cities had ever moved scrap on the Mississippi River.

Bundles of steel scrap ready for shipment at Davenport in 1958.

I I

Moving scrap by barge to St. Louis soon became an integral part of Alter's business, but the St. Louis scrap market was usually not as strong as some other more distant markets. I began thinking how profitable it would be to sell scrap to Pittsburgh, where the competition for scrap was always fierce. Pittsburgh was some 1,300 river miles from Davenport via the Mississippi River to Cairo, Illinois, then east on the Ohio River.

I asked American Commercial and Blaske Barge Lines for the ICC rate to Pittsburgh from Davenport. It was prohibitively high, so I did some investigating and discovered that rates to Pittsburgh from Memphis were much lower than from Davenport, even though the mileage was similar. I pointed this out to the barge lines and suggested they give me comparable rates. We finally negotiated a rate of about $8 per gross ton, a rate higher than I wanted but low enough for us to ship profitably to Pittsburgh.

The trouble was that the steel mills in St. Louis already looked on Alter as their own private resource, and they didn't want us moving scrap past their door to Pittsburgh. When they got wind of the deal, they put heavy pressure on the barge lines to rescind the rate reduction—and because the mills were bigger customers of the barge lines than we were, the barge lines had little option but to give in.

When I heard the news, I went up to Chicago to consult Ed Hayes, a maritime lawyer with Lord, Bissell, & Brook. Ed briefed me on Interstate Commerce Commision (ICC) regulations and assured me he'd take care of it. He sent a telegram to the ICC asking what had changed in the last two weeks so that the reduction was no longer justified, and the ICC promptly instructed the barge lines to honor their reduction, which they did. In truth, the barge lines were happy enough. They got the extra business and could pass all the blame on to the ICC. But I knew we'd never get another rate reduction from them. If we wanted further price cuts, we'd have to try something else.

In 1959, I met with a man who worked the Ohio and Tennessee Rivers with his towboat, and we calculated that by using his boat and renting some barges, we could cut $2 a gross ton from our trips to Pittsburgh. It seemed like a good idea, but when I asked Ed Hayes his opinion, he told me we'd be evading ICC law on nonbulk goods. The law was idiotic, but it existed, so we had to respect it. I asked Ed if he could think of an alternative.

"Sure," said Ed. "Buy yourself a towboat and some barges, put some river people on your payroll, and haul scrap in private carriage."

I told Ed that he was crazy. No one at Alter had the first idea how to run a barge line, least of all me. He told me to think about it anyway, and commented that if Alter did go into the barge business, we'd soon be hauling all kinds of goods and our barge operation would someday be huge. Later, my father said exactly the same thing. And boy, were they both right.

Dumb as the idea sounded, I couldn't get it out of my head, so I figured out how much it would cost to buy, maintain, and run a towboat and four barges. Then I made productivity and rate projections. The numbers looked promising, so I took them to Frank. After studying the numbers, he gave me authority to go ahead if I could get the financing. Frank had always given me freedom to work in whatever part of the business I wanted, but even so, when he allowed me to proceed, I was surprised. Despite all the growth he'd achieved, he was still a one-yard scrap dealer at heart, and to this day I have a sneaking suspicion that he never thought I'd get the financing. If so, he was very nearly right.

I took my forecasts and business plan on a tour of Iowa and Illinois banks, but nobody would lend me the money. Looking back, I don't blame them. After all, I was a thirty-year-old kid with no experience in the barge business. They must have thought I was crazy. Finally, I visited Gene Hawkinson at Central Life Assurance in Des Moines, who had already financed barges for Peabody Coal and so felt comfortable with them. Gene grilled me for two tough hours, then finally agreed to finance four barges. Finally, I was making progress, but without a towboat my efforts were useless.

I went back to see V.O. Figge at Davenport Bank & Trust. V.O. Figge was our primary banker, and when I told him I'd lined up barge financing but still couldn't find anybody to lend me money for a towboat, he agreed to the loan—but only if I could get Frank's signature on a guarantee. I went back to Frank, expecting he'd tell me no, but he surprised me for the second time by signing the guarantee.

At last, I had the financing in place. Now I just needed a boat, some barges, and some business.

III

The M/V *Keystone* was a good, solid, boat. Built by Dravo's marine division in 1945, it had been operating for their sand and gravel division in the Pittsburgh area. When I heard it was for sale, I had it examined for value and condition by a marine surveyor, then bought it for $125,000 and renamed it the M/V *Frank R. Alter*. I also bought four used open-hopper barges for $30,000 each. I didn't want to bring empty barges back to Davenport, so I called on Tody Fair, General Manager of Eastern Iowa Light & Power's new power plant at Montpelier, Iowa, some fifteen miles downriver from Davenport, and offered to deliver coal for him at a rate slightly discounted from those of the established barge lines. Courageously, Tody took a chance on us.

On its maiden voyage for us, the *Frank* moved light boat down the Ohio River from Pittsburgh to Jeffersonville, Indiana, picked up our four used barges, then pushed them up the Green River in Kentucky. The barges were loaded with coal, then pushed to Montpelier, Iowa. It took four days to unload the coal, and every night the *Frank* pushed one barge upriver to the Davenport seawall for loading with scrap to be taken to Pittsburgh.

Frank Alter stands alongside Alter Company's first towboat, named in his honor.

It was spring, and the river was running high and swift. Jimmy, *Frank's* captain, was a veteran of the Ohio River but had little experience on the much tougher Mississippi, so I hired a local pilot to advise him. The second night after the boat and barges left for Pittsburgh, Renee and I had some friends over for a party. Halfway through the evening, our telephone rang.

"Bernie," came a southern voice, "this is Jimmy. Jimmy on the *Frank. R. Alter.*"

"Yes, Jimmy. Is everything okay?"

"Fine," said Jimmy. "Everything's just fine. There's just one little problem."

"What?"

"Well, we're down here at Lock and Dam 22, and we hit the lock wall."

"You did what? Is anybody hurt?"

"No, everyone's fine."

"What about the boat?"

"It's fine. There's just a little bit of damage to one of the barges."

"A little damage? How little?"

"It done sunk," said Jimmy.

I felt like someone had hit me in the stomach with an iron fist. How was I going to explain this one away? Later, I learned that the pilot had warned Jimmy not to take more than two barges through the lock at a time, but Jimmy and his grandpa had ignored his advice and gone ahead with all four. Thanks to his recklessness, we now had $30,000 of barge and 1,200 gross tons of scrap lying on the river bottom.

Thankfully, our insurers put us in contact with a salvage company, who located the barge, right side up, under forty feet of water. The salvage company picked up the scrap with a waterproof magnet and reloaded it onto a rented barge. In fact, when we delivered the recovered scrap, we'd added twelve tons to the net weight! Our insurance premiums went up, but the episode wasn't as costly as it might have been, especially when the Corps of Engineers accepted the abandonment of the old barge underwater. We'd sunk our barge, all right, but not our barge company.

I V

Despite that narrow escape, we were having problems of a different kind. Under Jimmy's captaincy, our towboat and barges were not meeting my projections, not by a nautical mile. Even though we'd won good backhaul business, pushing scrap down to St. Louis and Pittsburgh and bringing coal back from west Kentucky or southern Illinois to Montpelier or La Crosse, our ton-mileage was a big disappointment. Our operation was losing money, and Frank wasn't the kind to let that go on for long.

I decided I had to replace Jimmy, but I had no idea who to replace him with, so I took the problem to Saul Greenstein. Saul moved tallow downriver and brought molasses back up to Dubuque, and he knew far more than I did about the barging

*Eno Dupuis, one of the finest captains on the
inland waterways system.*

business (not a difficult accomplishment at the time). He put me in touch with Eno
Dupuis, a Cajun boat owner from Breaux Bridge, Louisiana, who moved oil for the
Ashland Oil Company out of Ashland, Kentucky. Eno was one of the finest captains on
the inland waterway system, and I gave him a call. Saul had already briefed him, and
Eno told me not to worry, he'd take care of our problems. He did, too. He installed a
new captain, Sambo Dean, and a new pilot. Both were Cajun. Sambo then stripped all
the trimmings off the boat, took the benches off the decks, tore down the awnings, and
tossed them all overboard.

"This is now a work boat," he announced.

First stop was Cairo, Illinois, for a partial crew change. When the fresh crew heard
about Sambo, they refused to come aboard. They didn't want anything to do with
really hard work. Within two weeks, *Frank's* entire crew was Cajun. They drank
chicory coffee, ate crawfish, and put productivity up thirty percent. Boat and barges
immediately started earning profits, and with great relief I assured Frank we'd be okay.

The episode taught me a big lesson about management. Projections and numbers
are fine and necessary, but unless you get the right people doing the right job at the
right time, they mean nothing. Eno Dupuis was the right guy at the right time, and

without him Alter Barge Line would never have survived. He left us after just one year, sadly, because Ashland Oil demanded he work on his *Cotton Queen* full-time. But Eno was never the kind to leave a friend in the lurch, and he promised to find us a replacement better than himself. As always, he was as good as his word. He found us Gordon Jones.

If Eno had been great for us, Gordon was better. The truth was, Eno had a major character flaw: he was way too helpful to other people. Every time anyone was in trouble, they'd give Eno a call, as I'd done, and he'd come through for them. Once he even failed to return our chartered barges because he rushed off to help a friend.

Gordon Jones joined Alter Barge Line in 1961.

The Gordon Jones *was named to mark Gordon's outstanding contributions to Alter Barge Line.*

Gordon Jones was a great guy too, but he was also a good businessman and understood responsibility.

Gordon and I hired Bob Gardner as port captain, and Bob took over hiring crew members. Bob was from Kentucky, and he hired mostly from Kentucky and Tennessee. The numbers of our Cajun crew members gradually diminished to none. It was inevitable, because crews tended to enjoy working with people from the same background, but the towboats lost some of their color and a lot of spice from the menu.

The new crews were terrific workers, though, and they took great pride in their boats. An ex-U.S. Navy captain once came aboard an Alter boat and remarked nostalgically that we ran our boats the same way the Navy used to run theirs. Our boats were the cleanest and best maintained on the river. They were also among the most efficient.

One time, the U.S. Coast Guard unintentionally did its best to break up our crews. The Coast Guard's licensing system had slipped out of date, and licenses were only required for crew on steam-powered towboats, of which there were about two left on the entire inland waterways system. Now the Coast Guard wanted to license crews on diesel towboats. Suddenly, our pilots, engineers, mates, and other crew needed to pass written tests. That was a serious problem. Although they knew the inland waterways system like the backs of their hands, many of them couldn't read or write very well. Others had no idea how to answer exam questions or take a test. They were understandably afraid of losing their livelihoods.

Gordon Jones and I hired temporary replacements for our towboats, then sent our people to a new school in Blytheville, Arkansas. For the next four days, they learned how to take a test, what type of questions to expect, and how to answer them. That Friday, the Coast Guard conducted a half-day of rigorous testing. To everyone's delight, and thanks to their hard work, all of our people passed. For the rest of the day, they celebrated in proper style.

Incidentally, I didn't think much of that first test. Renee and I owned a small pleasure boat back then, and we'd taken some lessons from the Power Squadron to learn about safety and the rules of the river. It was a good course, and I'd recommend it for anyone operating a pleasure boat. As a result, I could answer 90 percent of the questions on the Coast Guard test. Did that mean I considered myself qualified to captain a towboat? No way. It was stupid to think that a written test alone could determine a pilot's or engineer's capability. Today, fortunately, the Coast Guard also requires experience on the river before it hands out licenses.

V

Our new baling machinery at the Davenport yard was producing a whole new kind of scrap bundle. These bundles, produced by baling a whole car without the motor block, weighed about 2,500 pounds each and measured 24" X 25" X 60". They could not readily be used by Northwestern Steel and Wire in Sterling because, as the scrap melted in its electric furnace, the heavy bundles could fall sideways against an electrode and break it. These bundles were ideal for open hearth furnaces such as Laclede's in Alton, Illinois. Mr. Paul Akin told us to barge them down and Laclede's would chew them up. Those furnaces chewed up many thousands of tons, until the day one of our bundles pushed another through the rear wall of their furnace. It seemed an appropriate time to look for a new customer, and we soon found one—in Mexico.

In 1960, we printed some marketing brochures for our scrap and transport businesses, and they proved a great asset to our selling efforts, showing how our two arms could pull together to benefit our customers. The next year, Renee and I traveled to Mexico. It was part holiday, but it was also an opportunity for me to visit one of the world's most aggressively expanding steel scrap markets. I stopped off in Monterrey, Mexico City, and Brownsville, Texas, to talk to some iron and steel people and ship-stevedoring companies. For two years, we heard nothing, and it seemed my trip had been unproductive. Then a Mexican intermediary called. He'd picked up one of our brochures from a stevedore in Brownsville and was wondering if we could supply scrap to a steel mill in Monclova, northwest of Monterrey.

The mill wanted huge quantities of scrap and seemed prepared to pay good prices, so Chuck Smith and I hired a plane and a pilot and flew down to Brownsville to meet the intermediary and a steel mill representative. It was a long flight and a small plane. By the time we reached Brownsville, Chuck and I were both squeezing our knees, aching for a bathroom. The intermediary was waiting for us on the tarmac, along with the steel mill purchasing agent, who looked for all the world like Pancho Villa with his sombrero, huge mustache, and riding breeches. But we were too desperate to say much, and we ran straight past them into the bathroom. To our surprise, the intermediary happily followed us. "Good," he said. "I wanted to talk to you alone. I want to fix my commission. And I don't want the steel company knowing how much it is."

This was all new to me. I took a figure off the top of my head. "You're getting 50 cents a ton," I told him, while busy with other things in the bathroom. "And the mill's going to know."

"But I wanted $2 a ton," he complained.

"Our plane's still outside," I reminded him. "We'll get back on it if you want." He was wise enough to figure out that 50 cents a ton on something was better than $2 a ton on nothing, and agreed. He introduced us to Mauro Villareal, buyer for Monclova's Altos Hornos Steel. Altos Hornos (Tall Horns—named for their huge chimneys) had just split from its previous scrap broker and was looking for 20,000 tons of baled scrap to start, going up to 50,000 tons. It was an enormous amount, by far the biggest deal Chuck and I had ever been involved in.

Mauro didn't want to negotiate at the airport. He wanted us to meet Señor Pape, his boss, and other representatives of their mill. We flew on into Mexico. It was a hairy flight. The mountains were higher than our charts indicated, but we squeaked over. After four days of waiting, we finally got to meet Señor Pape. Harold Pape, it turned out, was an expatriate American, a steel man from Fort Wayne, Indiana, who'd gone to Mexico to try his luck with a steel mill and had prospered.

Pape studied the deal, approved it, then casually advised us that payment terms were one year. It was a bad shock. There was no way Alter could risk that kind of exposure. Chuck and I glanced at each other, the biggest deal of our lives falling apart. I told Pape that our normal terms were thirty days, but Pape told us not to worry. All we had to do was calculate a year's interest and add it to the cost of the scrap. He'd then give us a commercial note which we could take to one of a number of American banks they used, where the note would be discounted for cash. We looked through the bank list and saw Continental Illinois, out of Chicago, a bank we used. We had a deal.

We flew back to the United States later that night, landing in Texarkana, Arkansas. The pilot, Chuck, and I found a bar where the manager thought one peso was equivalent to one dollar, whereas in fact the peso was worth only a fraction of a dollar. We paid for our drinks in ten peso notes, and the staff kept bringing us our change in dollars. It was the finest exchange system I've come across in many years of traveling, and we converted so many pesos that I could barely remember the end of the evening.

We baled our first bundles in our Harris 3000 machine at Davenport, and the Altos Hornos furnaces seemed to like them. Soon, our Davenport yard could no longer satisfy their voracious appetite. We sent scrap from La Crosse and St. Paul, then started buying from dealers in Louisville, Memphis, Nashville, Ashland, and Cincinnati, and barging down to Brownsville, where we loaded it onto railroad cars. The scrap was so precious that the Mexicans even put armed guards on top of the cars to deter bandits.

Mexico was not our only international venture. The Mississippi River, the intercoastal waterways, and the Panama Canal had also opened Europe and the Far East to us. Japan, in particular, was desperate for ferrous scrap at the time. In one early deal, we sold 10,000 gross tons of #2 bundles to Kanematsu, a Japanese importer. That was eight bargeloads, and the *Frank* pushed them downstream from the Davenport yard. It was as much as the boat could handle, and the trip proved so stressful that the pilot resigned the moment he stepped ashore at New Orleans.

The Frank R. Alter, *Alter's first towboat.*

I was almost as anxious as the pilot, but for a different reason. The scrap was to be loaded onto an ocean-going ship at New Orleans, and we needed the barges at the port the moment the ship arrived or we'd owe a fortune in demurrage. I flew down to Louisiana, went directly to the Royal Orleans Hotel in the French Quarter, took my binoculars onto the roof, and focused them on the docks. The very first thing I saw was our ship lowering anchor. The second thing I saw was the *Frank* pushing eight barges downstream. We'd all arrived at exactly the same time.

The stevedore company slid the heavy scrap bundles down chutes into the hold, and two days later the ship set sail for the Panama Canal and Japan. After he'd unloaded, the ship's owner called, mad as could be. It seemed that in loading the scrap, the bundles had accelerated down the chutes and shot out across the hold like missiles, crashing into the sides of the ship and causing serious internal damage. I had to remind him that we'd sold the bundles free on board, and that loading them onto the ship was therefore his problem, not ours.

Some time later, we moved a shipment of steel turnings downstream. The turnings were covered in oil and therefore flammable, so when we transferred them into the hold of the ship, I warned the captain that if they started to smoke, he shouldn't douse them with sea water. Salt would only set off a reaction and aggravate the situation. Of course, as soon as the captain saw some smoke coming from the hold, he ignored my warning and pumped in sea water, and the turnings promptly started to smolder badly. He was a brave guy, though, because he still sailed across the Pacific to Tokyo, despite the fire. It took three months for the ship to cool down so that it could be unloaded. Again (thank God!), it wasn't our responsibility, as we'd sold free on board New Orleans and had warned the buyers about the possibility of something like this happening.

V I

Two other incidents from the early days of the Alter Barge Line need recording. The first was a fatal tragedy; the second was no more than a financial setback.

It was summer 1961, and we'd moored two barges against the Davenport seawall while we loaded them with scrap iron. One night, the two barges got loose and floated free into the center of the Mississippi River. The night was coal-black, and some people were out joyriding in a speedboat. Tragically, they crashed into the barges. Two were killed and two more badly injured.

I hurried down to the seawall as soon as I heard. It didn't occur to me then to worry about Alter's legal liability, but the next morning the lawyers started calling. They soon filed suit, asking for the kind of huge damages that would bankrupt our company. We turned to our insurers, but our policies apparently covered us only when our barges were being pushed by a boat or were secured to the seawall. Neither was the case here. It looked as if we were finished.

We were saved by an extraordinary and ironic coincidence. A year or two earlier, I'd bought a policy from an agent of Mel Foster Insurance. The policy had a clause in it which, while far from conclusive, gave us a point of argument. The irony was that the agent who'd sold me the policy wasn't around to clarify the clause; he'd been one of the two people killed in the speedboat accident.

We also argued that we'd not been negligent. It had been a calm night with little current. The mooring ropes on the barges were intact and were actually coiled on the gunwale of the barge. We'd been having problems with vandals. I believed then, and I believe now, that some kids set the barges loose as a prank, but there was no way I could prove it. There was a third angle to our defense, too. The people injured and killed had contributed to the tragedy by driving a speedboat recklessly on a dark night while drunk.

We negotiated hard and finally reached a compromise with the lawyers and our insurance company, under which we paid $300,000. It was a heavy price, but at least we could stay in business. We learned from it, too, and checked and double-checked our mooring cables

The Mississippi River flooded farmland around Davenport, Iowa, every few years.

every night after that. And another item won more serious scrutiny after that night: our insurance policies. We started using marine insurer Robert Ackerburg, a move that proved to be the beginning of an outstanding relationship.

The second incident occurred in 1965. Alter barges were bringing salt up from Louisiana and storing it in the seawall yard for trucking to stores along local highways, for salting roads in snow and ice storms. In the spring of that year, the Mississippi River flooded at Davenport and spilled over the seawall into our yard. I was out of town at the time, and one of our people decided that, above all else, we should keep our crane safe and dry, so he drove it up on top of one of the salt piles.

By the time I returned to the yard, I saw we had a problem. The flooding river was eating away the salt pile, and the crane on top was already leaning at a precarious thirty-degree angle, about to topple over. Clayton Grass brought a rowboat over, and thankfully managed to get the crane down off the salt pile into the water before it fell over. The flood subsided shortly afterwards, but by that time, all the salt, except for a little residue whitewashing the ground, was on its way back to Louisiana.

CHAPTER SEVEN
YARDS

By 1961, our boat and barges were leading our scrap business in some unanticipated directions. We were doing such regular trade up in Wisconsin and Minnesota that we decided to invest in our own private facilities. George Jollivette had a coal yard on the La Crosse, Wisconsin, riverfront, and I arranged to use it for loading and unloading scrap and coal. Steve Rupsch went up to La Crosse and set up an office in an old house on a corner of the yard. We'd just unloaded our first shipment of coal and were about to load it with scrap when the Mississippi Valley Barge Line sent us a furious telegram. Barge line officials claimed that they, not George Jollivette, owned the dock and threatened to sue us if we loaded so much as a pound of scrap. George then admitted that Mississippi Valley did own the dock, so we had to truck our scrap several miles to a public dock. That, obviously, was no long-term solution, so we took some riverfront property of our own, pinned two old scrap barges to the riverbed, one on top of the

Unloading salt at Alter's La Crosse yard.

other, and made ourselves a very cheap but beautifully effective dock. The facility grew quickly and was soon a scrap yard in its own right. It also handled coal and salt.

Our relationship with George Jollivette didn't go so well. George had a partner in Davenport, Bob Clarno, who stored coal at our Davenport seawall yard, then sold it to Quad Cities' businesses. One day, I arrived at our riverfront terminal to see his coal surrounded with yellow signs that claimed the coal was the property of the West Kentucky Coal Company. Apparently, George had bought the coal from West Kentucky but hadn't paid for it yet. He hadn't paid me for freight either, and if he was struggling for money, I wanted to be first in line. So I removed the West Kentucky signs and claimed first lien. West Kentucky grumbled a bit, but even their lawyers admitted I was entitled to the lien since the coal was on my property and in my possession.

That was the last time we did business with George.

II

Our second remote yard was in St. Paul, Minnesota. The Twin Cities region was one of the Mississippi River's major shipping areas, and we were soon doing a profitable business there. We'd take coal up from Kentucky or salt from Louisiana and bring scrap down to New Orleans for sale to Commercial Metals or Southern Scrap, who'd put it on their ocean-going ships for export. At first, as in La Crosse, we used the public docks for loading and unloading. Our boat and barges were far too often waiting around for docks and cranes or storage facilities, so in late 1961 we leased a stretch of riverfront property in St. Paul and used it as a marine terminal, as well as for storage and scrap processing. Alan Levey took charge of the facility in 1965 and ran it for many years.

Incidentally, Alan used to tell a good story about Frank, which showed how sharp Frank was with details, even though Alter had become a lot larger. One time Alan wanted a new pickup truck for the St. Paul yard. He knew it wouldn't be easy to persuade Frank to okay the purchase, so he came down to Davenport and called on Frank in his office.

Hydraulic guillotine shear at Alter's St. Paul plant.

"Frank," said Alan, "I've got a problem. My pickup truck is falling apart and my guys are breaking down every six blocks, and that's bad for our reputation and bad for business." He proceeded to list all the truck's faults, exaggerating how bad a state it was in, making out that he kept it running only with a combination of string, ingenuity, and prayer. "I need a new truck," concluded Alan, throwing up his hands. "This one is scrap on wheels."

"What do you mean, scrap on wheels?" Frank replied, heatedly. "If it's scrap on wheels, why in hell did you put in a new carburetor and two new shocks last month?" Without even glancing at his records, Frank began to recite a list. "You had

Alan Levey, former manager of Alter's St. Paul yard.

the engine rebuilt just three months ago," he continued. "And only last year, you had new tires put on. What do you mean, scrap? It's not scrap, and you're not getting a new truck." Alan ducked out of Frank's office in a hurry. He couldn't believe that Frank could recall off the top of his head the exact repairs that had been done a year earlier to a pickup truck in a remote yard. Now he knew better.

St. Paul did fine for a few years, but then North Star Steel opened a mill nearby and set up their own scrap-buying operation. They changed their bid prices only once a month, while the market changed several times a week. That meant that the local peddlers took horrible advantage of them, but it also meant that our St. Paul yard struggled to compete. Later, Cargill acquired North Star Steel and continued the policy. One day, a Cargill vice president came to visit me in Davenport and asked how on earth we'd managed to keep our relationships with John Deere and our other customers for so long. Didn't they realize they could do better by brokering the scrap for themselves? I explained all the benefits we brought to the table: experience, skill, service, controlled chemistry, quality control, on-hand inventory. I also mentioned that we provided all these benefits and yet were still cheaper than if our customers did it in-house.

"But why would they let you make a profit out of them?" he insisted.

He couldn't understand that John Deere and our other customers used us because we made their business better. Today, outsourcing is widely accepted as a crucial component of successful management. Those mills that don't accept that view, and insist on brokering their own scrap, simply wind up paying more.

III

Our yards in La Crosse and St. Paul were our first real experiments with managing multiple yards. At the time, remote yards were rare in the scrap industry, if not unique, and pioneering had its problems. The first challenge was to find good people to run the yards. It wasn't easy. I knew that people were either intelligent or dumb, hard-working or lazy, but it took me a while to learn that the most dangerous manager wasn't the dumb, lazy person, as you'd think, but the conscientious dummy. A lazy manager doesn't do enough to cause much trouble, but the hard-working idiot will spend all day wreaking havoc.

I also learned some telltale signs to look for when hiring people. For one thing, I stopped hiring pipe smokers. Cigarette smokers were fine: they could do six things at the same time and still find room for a cigarette. But pipe smokers spent half their day tamping on their darn pipes, deliberating on their darn pipes, cleaning out their darn pipes, and never getting anything done.

Once we'd hired the right managers, we needed to make them understand what they were in business to achieve. Although I'd had no formal business or economic training, I tried over the years to give our people a simple idea of the financial workings of the scrap industry, so I devised two equations. They were:

$V \times M - C = P$ (Volume multiplied by Margin less Costs equals Profit); and

$P / I = ROI$ (Profit over Investment equals Return of Investment).

I used these two equations over and over again with Alter managers to give them a sense of what they needed to do to make money. The equations worked well for scrap, and I later found they worked in all forms of business too.

We also needed to coordinate our efforts, maximize sales, and maintain quality, while keeping one eye on our consolidated accounts and the other on making sure we weren't cutting each other's throats by competing for business. That demanded new management and communications systems. With the help of Frank, Chuck Smith, and McGladrey & Pullen, our local accountants, we set up a sophisticated system of financial controls and instituted management training programs. We also computerized stock and quality control—although our first move into computerization was an admitted disaster. Our card-index IBM crashed as regularly as a car test dummy. We grew to hate it so

Alter's first computer was an IBM 650 data processing system.

much that during a managers meeting in Davenport, we took it down to the parking lot, handed out sledgehammers, and encouraged our managers to put their heartfelt frustrations into smashing it flat. Thankfully, our next system proved more efficient.

We also devised some new incentive schemes. We gave generous bonuses to yard managers, calculated half on corporate profits and half on the profits of their own yards. We also instituted annual awards of Krugerrands and other gold coins for the best run, most improved, and most profitable yards. The gold awards soon became very highly prized, as much for the achievements they represented as for their intrinsic value.

IV

Unlike our moves to La Crosse and St. Paul, Alter's 1962 expansion into Council Bluffs, Iowa, was not driven by our barge business but by the needs of a new customer. I was in St. Louis one day and stopped in to see a friend, a trader who worked for David Joseph, one of the country's largest scrap brokers. He greeted me with a broad grin on his face and boasted he'd just sneaked in our back door and made his first sale to the new Griffin plant.

"Griffin?" I asked. "Which plant?"

"At Council Bluffs."

I hadn't heard anything about a new plant in Council Bluffs, and I had never heard of Griffin either. That worried me. After congratulating my friend, I headed back to Davenport and asked Chuck Smith about it. He knew nothing either, so we called in Steve Rupsch, who covered that territory for us. Steve said that maybe Griffin was converting an old, empty, railroad-wheel factory on the outside of town. He checked and sure enough, Griffin Wheel had become Griffin Pipe and planned to make cast iron pipe. That was great news since the company would be using huge volumes of scrap. Now we just had to make sure Griffin bought it from us.

After arranging an appointment with Sam Prest, one of Griffin's officers, Chuck put together an impressive presentation, including a map color-coded with so many pins it looked like a porcupine. Chuck's tactic was to make the map too

Alter Company Leases 10-Acre Site In Bluffs For A New Plant

The Alter Co., with headquarters at Davenport, announced Wednesday it has leased a 10-acre site here and will begin district plant operations later this year.

The firm is a large processor and broker of iron and steel scrap and is a major producer of nickel base alloys and foundry ferro alloys.

The operation here will deal with breaking down scrap metal for delivery to foundries and steel mills in Iowa, Nebraska and Missouri. No smelting operations are planned here.

Selects Architect

The plant will be located on a site, obtained from the Union Pacific Railroad, south of the Griffin Pipe Products Co. at 2601 Ninth Ave.

L. T. Carrithers of Council Bluffs has been named architect for a project which will involve the construction of an office building, a warehouse and installation of production machinery.

Frank Alter, president of the company, met with Mayor Leon Morse and Chamber of Commerce officials Wednesday at Hotel Chieftain.

8 To 10 Employes

Alter said the operation probably would start with 8 to 10 employes.

"I hope someday that it will be a 35-40 employe operation," he said.

"We feel that this is a good part of the country to locate," he added. The company has other officers and plants at LaCrosse, Wis., Detroit, Mich.; Minneapolis, Minn.; Winona, Minn.; Amsterdam, Holland, and Milan, Italy.

Plant Location . . . of the Alter Co. is discussed by Mayor Leon Morse, Frank Alter, head of the firm, and W. D. Cairney, Chamber of Commerce president.

In 1963, Alter made news with its new plant in Council Bluffs.

Griffin Pipe Products' plant at Council Bluffs, Iowa.

big to file and too beautiful to trash, so that Sam would have to keep it out on view. Griffin was still building when Chuck and Steve arrived, so they met Sam Prest out in a hallway for a few minutes. Sam didn't hold out much hope for us, as he'd already identified his probable scrap supplier right across the Missouri River. Then Sam told them he had pressing business elsewhere and had to go. As they were parting, Chuck forced the presentation map on Sam as a keepsake. Then he returned to Davenport and waited, not very optimistically, for a response.

Three weeks later, out of the blue, Frank got a call from Sam Prest. "Hey," asked Sam, "I've got this huge map sitting on my desk. It's driving me crazy. Tell me, what on earth do all these yellow pins stand for?"

We were in.

Sam sent his buyer, Orris Dean, on a tour of possible scrap suppliers. When Orris came down to Davenport, Chuck put him up in a local hotel and arranged for us all to meet in the morning. As we were going in to meet Orris for breakfast, Chuck took me aside and, in a whisper, asked me to order a glass of warm orange juice.

"What?"

"Please," said Chuck. "Do it."

Well, we introduced ourselves and sat down. The waitress came, and I ordered two eggs, some toast, and a glass of orange juice. I wanted it warm, not cold.

Orris looked at me in open-mouthed astonishment, as if we were on daytime TV together and I'd just revealed I was his long-lost brother. "You drink warm orange juice?" he asked.

"All my life," I lied.

"I thought I was the only one," said Orris. "I thought I was the only person in the world to drink warm orange juice." That was typical Chuck. He'd always take the extra step to create a personal bond with our customers. More important, he knew creating a bond wasn't enough. He knew how to keep it too, by providing good value and service.

After breakfast, the real business came under discussion. We desperately wanted to broker scrap for Griffin, and I suggested to Chuck that we take a low commission to ensure we won the business, maybe 75 cents or $1 for each gross ton we brokered. But Chuck told me to let him handle the negotiations, and he got us $1 for every *net* ton.

A gross ton was 2,240 pounds, while a net ton was just 2,000 pounds. That was 12 percent more than I'd wanted to ask for, and it was the moment I knew Chuck was a better deal-maker than I was. He knew scrap, of course, and the numbers. But his secret was that he liked people. He was truly interested in them, their kids, and their hobbies. Our customers realized he was genuine, through and through, and they couldn't help but like him. They couldn't resist him. Chuck became Alter's number one trader, and he was terrific at it.

One winter, we almost got into trouble with Griffin. A sudden snap of bad weather closed down the railroads, and we couldn't ship the scrap iron we had promised, which was waiting at our yard. Griffin was getting desperate. It was Friday. If they didn't get delivery by Monday, they'd have to close the foundry, a significant financial setback. Sunday came, and thankfully the railroad started to move again. We just beat our deadline.

After that, Griffin agreed it would be smart to have a supply of scrap on hand for bad weather or railroad strikes. We set up a ten-acre holding yard just behind Griffin's Council Bluffs factory and hired a manager from the East to run the yard. His pedigree was so impressive he'd have won "Best of Show" if he'd been a poodle, but he never got his job done. When I went to the Bluffs to find out why, I spoke to the local peddlers and auto wreckers, and they told me that they weren't going to do business with "that stuck-up SOB." We began looking around for someone new.

In our early days barging scrap, we'd rented land on the Illinois River from a small sand and gravel company in Peru, Illinois, and Frank had agreed that I could hire my Aunt Sonia's husband, Nate Curtis, as manager. Nate built up a good business, buying scrap from peddlers, then loading it on to barges with a small crane. Peru never became a big operation, but Nate made sure it always made a little money. One Saturday morning, a peddler brought a truckload of scrap into the yard. The crane operator was not in that morning, so Nate unloaded it himself. Tragically, he didn't know how to operate the crane properly, and it began to tilt and topple. Nate jumped the wrong way, and the crane fell on him and killed him. We closed the yard at once, but Aunt Sonia never forgave Frank, or me.

My uncle, Nate Curtis, was manager of our Peru, Illinois, yard.

Jake Barnes led Council Bluffs into becoming Alter's finest scrap yard.

The peddler who'd brought the load into Nate's yard that tragic morning was Jake Barnes. Jake had been raised into the scrap business, working for his uncle's yard in Mendota, Illinois. He'd expected to make partner, but it never happened. By 1963, he'd given up hope, and I hired him to run a small portable baler in the Bluffs area. Now, when we needed a new manager at Council Bluffs, I asked Jake to take charge until I found someone else. I didn't look very hard or for very long, however, because Jake soon proved himself our best manager. He had the right attitude. Every time he looked at the sign in the Council Bluffs yard, he saw his own name on it, not Alter's, and that

Alter's scrap yard at Council Bluffs, Iowa.

gave him intense pride. He doted on the Council Bluffs yard like a mother with her first child, and he built it into Alter's most profitable yard and one of the finest scrap yards in the country.

Jake never went to college, and that bugged him all his life. He developed a complex about his lack of formal education, which was a real shame. He never did realize that while you may need to be smart to go to college (although I've met a few who aren't even that!), you don't need to go to college to be smart. Jake was living proof: he won so many Krugerrands in our annual awards he could have stocked the gold reserve of most small countries.

College education or not, he always knew what needed to be done. He got along terrifically both with the local peddlers and with the people he sold to. He bought the best new equipment and got the most out of it. He also got the best out of the people he employed, because he knew how to handle them and believed that people could do anything if they tried hard enough. He also made sure his employees followed safety procedures. Jake weighed about 300 pounds, and if he saw one of his people without safety toe shoes on, he would "accidentally" step on their toes. Those employees would never forget their safety shoes again.

Soon he was producing more volume than Griffin could handle and was selling scrap to Kansas City, Missouri, Norfolk, Nebraska, and elsewhere. Despite working long hours, Jake still found time to become deeply involved with the Council Bluffs community. He helped establish the Council Bluffs Business Association, helped with charities, and got on excellently with local business and political leaders.

In January 1994, Jake was preparing to hand over his Council Bluffs yard to his successor and enjoy his richly deserved retirement when he died. It was a terrible blow to his family and to his many, many friends.

CHAPTER EIGHT
RELATIONSHIPS

With Jake Barnes in charge of Council Bluffs, our relationship with Griffin quickly grew strong. Not all Griffin people were immediately sold on us, however. Frank Marold, one of Griffin's officers, had been working on the East Coast where he developed a deep suspicion of scrap dealers. But as the weeks, months, and years rolled by, and we kept supplying quality scrap at very competitive rates, even he came around.

His conversion was so complete that when he later transferred to Chicago as a vice president of Griffin's national operations, he suggested we set up yards next to all Griffin's other sites around the country. We looked at the idea and brokered a few deals, but outside of the Midwest, we could never guarantee the level of service we wanted for the right price, so we limited our relationship with Griffin to Council Bluffs.

Relationships with leading foundries and steel mills had always been a key part of Alter's growth. Now they were critical. With our multiple yards, we needed to buy and sell tens of thousands of tons of scrap every month just to meet our overhead, and that made it vital for us to keep on good terms with our major accounts. At the same time, a new generation of managers was coming into American industry, and they didn't want presents slipped to them under the table. They wanted fair dealing, professionalism, and reliability. They wanted suppliers they could trust, so that when they verified scrap weights on neutral scales, they knew they'd been paying honest prices.

That suited us just fine. Alter had always acted with total integrity and honesty, and now we found that those qualities were helping us to achieve tremendous growth and success, as exemplified in Quincy, Illinois. Gardner Denver, a Quincy company, used to buy scrap almost exclusively from a local dealer who'd bullied the purchasing manager into believing he was the only trustworthy supplier in the region. Whenever anyone else made deliveries, that local dealer would scorn its quality and claim that whoever delivered it was cheating Gardner Denver. If anything, the opposite was true, but the slander worked its trick, and the purchasing manager often returned the scrap deliveries that the local dealer identified as inferior. That cost the brokers a fortune in freight and was as annoying as hell, so most of them simply stopped doing business with Gardner Denver.

Barges being pushed to Quincy, Illinois in 1961.

Then E. E. Groves took over as purchasing manager. At first, he let things go on as before, but then Chuck paid him a courtesy call. Groves asked Chuck why Alter never tried to sell scrap to Gardner Denver any more. Chuck told him bluntly about the reputation Gardner Denver had earned itself. This news came as such a shock that Groves spoke immediately to Schumaker, vice president of foundries. As a result, Schumaker asked us to submit a proposal for supplying them with cast iron scrap.

"Fine," we replied, "but only if you give us the exclusive contract."

Gardner Denver took a chance on us, and at once its productivity shot ahead. In fact, the improvement was so impressive that they asked us to supply their steel scrap, too. Word raced around Quincy's top industrialists that we were honest brokers, and soon we were invited to bid on Electric Wheel's scrap. We worked out everything from bin placement to collection schedules, but since we knew the purchasing manager was already buying from the scrap yard where his son worked, we weren't overly optimistic. To no one's surprise, the purchasing manager rejected our bid. But he was overruled, and we were awarded a trial contract, which evolved into a successful, long-term relationship. Then Maytag and Tonka Toys both asked us to bid for their business, and we won both accounts. We'd taken every industrial account in Quincy worth having. That was the power of reputation.

II

We'd do anything for our customers. Anything reasonable, that is. Chuck and I made sure our account people were always out on the road visiting customers, studying their foundries, furnaces, feeding systems, energy use, and products. Our visits had tangible benefits for our clients. Griffin Pipe, for example, used a charging box for their open-hearth furnace that could only take scrap two-feet wide or less. At our suggestion, Griffin increased its capacity by a foot, enabling the company to buy a cheaper grade of scrap. Over the years, that simple adjustment saved Griffin many millions of dollars.

Likewise, a steel mill in Guadalajara, Mexico, was recycling light scrap, not realizing that it took so much energy to melt that it was ruining the mills productivity. We gave company officials the correct specifications, and overnight they found they were melting fifty tons of steel scrap at a time rather than ten, with only a slight increase in energy costs.

We'd always try to solve our customers' problems where we could, even when we had no obligation to do so. In the early 1960s, John Deere began melting scrap steel at its Waterloo, Iowa, plant. Winter was coming, so the company ordered enough steel scrap to last through to spring and stored it in a craneway. The only problem was that Deere's inventory personnel had made a simple error in their survey. They hadn't factored in that steel was thirty pounds lighter a cubic foot than iron, and that meant they'd badly underestimated the amount of steel they needed.

John Deere's plant at Waterloo, Iowa.

January came, and Deere's buyers realized their stocks of scrap were running dangerously low, so they bought a consignment of steel scrap from a Chicago yard and had it shipped to Waterloo. When workers started to feed it into their furnace, though, it wouldn't melt properly. It was the wrong specification. Suddenly, Deere's buyers were the laughingstock of the scrap industry. Worse, they were in big trouble. Buying large quantities of scrap in the middle of winter is always expensive and sometimes impossible.

John Deere asked us to help and we agreed. The Armco Steel Mill in Kansas City, Missouri, was one of the Midwest's leading scrap consumers, and the mill was also buying scrap at the time. One Saturday morning, Chuck and I went to meet Armco's purchasing agent and one of its brokers and asked them to divert 4,000 tons of scrap to Waterloo, to see John Deere through the winter. When they refused, saying that it was Deere's problem, Chuck acquainted them with market dynamics. Farm tractors sold for more than new steel, he explained, and that meant Deere could outbid Armco if they had to. If we were forced to compete in the local market on Deere's behalf, the market could rise by $10 or $15 a ton, and Deere would still end up with the scrap. "Wouldn't it be easier to save everyone that trouble," said Chuck, "and just ship direct?" They both saw the force of Chuck's argument and diverted some cars already headed for Kansas City to Waterloo. The following summer, Deere officials recognized our help by asking us to buy and store scrap for them when the price was low, then to deliver it to them as needed during the winter.

In another example, Mexico was soon pulling so much scrap from the United States that our government decided to impose export quotas. The quotas pushed up the price of exported scrap, because everyone was fighting to buy it. To most dealers it was a profits bonanza, but at Alter we kept doing business with our long-term customers, charging them proper rates, making sure their mills and foundries were kept supplied. Again, we didn't make so much then as some of our speculating competitors, but when the quotas were lifted, our customers showed their appreciation by sending even more business our way. Yet again, our reputation had been justified, and enhanced.

Our extensive contacts were also useful. CF&I's steel mill in Pueblo, Colorado, depended on a huge brass screw nut for its operations, and it had broken. The screw nut was about a ton of solid brass, and it would take at least a month to get a new one from France, where the nuts were made. Until then, the mill would have to close. CF&I's purchasing manager was on the phone to Chuck, talking through his woes, when Chuck asked him if there weren't any screw nuts anywhere else in the world.

"Only one," replied the purchasing manager. "It's being held in stock by a Mexican mill."

"Mexico?" asked Chuck. "Where exactly?"

"Place called Altos Hornos, in Monclova," said the manager. "Their Number Two Plant has one. But that's no good to me."

"I know that plant," said Chuck. "It's run by Gabriel Magellon, a friend of mine. Let me give him a call."

Chuck reached Gabriel at once and learned that he'd just installed the new screw nut, but his old one still had some life in it. We'd done him some favors over the years, and he was happy as could be to sell it to us and transport it to the border, where CF&I gratefully picked it up. We even got them a good price.

Incidentally, with all the business we were doing with Altos Hornos, I thought it was a good idea to introduce Frank to Señor (Harold) Pape, so I persuaded him and Yetta to join Renee and me on one of our Mexican visits. After the four of us had checked into Acapulco's Pierre Hotel, I invited Pape to join us for dinner. He was living a luxurious life at the time, like a Mexican nobleman, and clearly enjoying it. He arrived for dinner with a beautiful young señorita on his arm, whom he introduced as his "treasurer's wife." Frank, who was very prudish and conservative, was really shocked. It made him so uncomfortable to see Pape flaunting his lifestyle that he could barely bring himself to talk. It was a horrible evening, although Pape didn't seem to mind much—in truth, he seemed to think the whole evening was very funny. I never asked Frank back to Mexico to meet with Harold Pape again, and he never asked to come.

CHAPTER NINE
ALTER AND ALLOY

Despite our blossoming scrap and barge business, not everything was coming up roses in the Alter garden. In truth, during the early 1960s, the company was becoming increasingly divided. Arant Sherman, my brother-in-law, and Marvin Pesses, his key vice president, had built Alter a significant nickel and nickel alloy business, buying and selling nickel-chrome and nickel-copper alloys such as stainless steel, then selling them to mills and foundries for the manufacture of jet engines and other hi-tech products.

As the nickel business grew, it gradually displaced Alter's other nonferrous business. Arant closed Frank's aluminum furnace and used the space for nickel alloys. He also commandeered the copper shot furnace. He did pretty well, too. For a while, Alter became the leading nickel alloy dealer in the Midwest. In fact, for a few years, I think it was the *only* nickel alloy dealer in the Midwest.

Arant had his own peculiar style of doing business, and it took his side of the company in a different direction from the rest of us. He did some really irritating things. He used to exaggerate how much money he was making, for example, which only made it tougher for all of us to cut deals. He even advertised as the world's largest dealer, which was embarrassing. He'd talk big, but increasingly, he'd act small. Some of the things he'd do were so petty they'd irritate the hell out of people. He used to accuse our bookkeeper of "reallocating" our profits and losses to make it appear that Alloy was losing money while scrap was making it. He even told his people not to keep Frank informed of what was going on. More and more often, Frank found himself pleading for peace. Once, he even flew off to Japan for a completely pointless visit, just to save Arant's face.

The situation would have been manageable had not some generous-spirited estate planning backfired. In an effort to avoid inheritance taxes, Frank had given up 90 percent of his company stock, either in gifts to his daughters or in sales at bargain prices to his sons-in-law. Arant and Anita now owned 45 percent, as did Renee and I. Frank owned only the remaining 10 percent.

Arant wanted to take control of the company, but I held that it was Frank's business for as long as he wanted it, whatever the stock position. The arguments grew worse. Arant proposed ideas that Frank couldn't stomach. When Frank rejected them, Arant complained bitterly that Frank never agreed to any of his schemes but was always prepared to finance mine. If there was truth in that, it was because Frank and I approached business from the same direction, while Arant had an approach all his own.

For example, strict control over spending had proved one of Alter's greatest strengths. If anyone ever bought an unnecessary monkey wrench, Frank would let him know all about it. But Arant didn't just want all the new monkey wrenches he could use, he wanted a company airplane. An airplane would have been hugely expensive, and we didn't need it, so Frank turned it down. Arant was unhappy. He asked George Otte, our treasurer, to justify the need for the airplane, but George replied that he couldn't. Arant then told George that he was not on his side, and George quit not long afterwards. Frank's refusal to buy the plane was the final straw for Arant. He came to me and told me that the old man had lost it. He suggested we pool our stock and vote to retire Frank off to Florida with a pension of $50,000 a year. Then, hinted Arant, the two of us could run things properly.

I told him no. It was Frank's business.

Arant didn't like that answer. Nickel alloy was having a good year, and he was feeling righteously frustrated with Frank and me. He retained a lawyer, Ralph Heninger, who threatened to bring suit on behalf of the minority shareholders, Anita and Arant, for mismanagement. Tension at the yard grew unbearably: it felt like the whole place was tearing in two. An unofficial Chinese Wall built up. Old friends didn't talk any more, and people fell ill with anxiety. When it grew so bad that even I considered leaving, I knew we had to find some resolution.

Frank still had the power to dismiss Arant, but he was too concerned for his grandchildren. Instead, I suggested we split the company and give the nickel alloy business to Arant. It was hard on Frank. After dedicating his life to building his company and his family, I was now asking him to split up both. He had no choice, however, and he finally agreed.

Advised by Margaret Stevenson, our attorney, I went head-to-head with Ralph Heninger for the negotiations. We slugged away like heavyweight boxers over a fifteen round prize fight and came out with a split decision—or, at least, a decision to split. Under the provisions of the thick stack of contractual agreements, the Davenport yard was physically sliced in two by a steel wire fence. For their 45 percent, Arant and Anita took all our cash, the nickel alloy business, and Alter's existing nonferrous scrap trade and steel warehousing. Frank and I kept the scrap yards, barges, and a mountain of debt. Financing our side of the deal wasn't easy, but V.O. Figge of Davenport Bank & Trust turned out to be a great help.

The deal struck, we were all relieved just to get on with our lives and our jobs. Within two years, we'd paid down our debt and were making good money again. All in all, it worked out okay for us at Alter Company.

I I

But Arant and Alloy didn't prosper so well. Marvin Pesses, an engineer with expertise in metallurgy and ceramics, was Arant's right hand man and key to the alloy business. He'd run a small aluminum foundry at his house before I'd asked him to join Alter. He had a wonderful brain for devising brilliant ideas. The only trouble was, he also had lots of crackpot schemes, and they were all but impossible to tell apart. Only Frank could confidently pick the gold nuggets from the iron sulfide.

When Marvin joined the nickel alloy business, he soon became its driving force. After the split, he asked Arant for the opportunity to buy stock in the venture, but Arant just laughed in his face. Marvin walked straight out and joined a company in Youngstown, Ohio. With its backing, he set up as a competitor to Alloy, with newer ideas, better equipment, and more energy. He also took a lot of Alloy's business with him. Alloy never made much progress after he left, and in fact went bankrupt in the mid 1980s, leaving its half of the yard an environmental mess, the soil clogged with pollutant minerals and littered with rusting drums filled with toxic chemicals.

But that's another story.

I I I

The family situation was not so good either. Frank and Yetta still kept in touch and visited their grandchildren every Sunday, but never without tension from Arant and Anita. It was heart wrenching to see Frank and Yetta so upset. They were such good and kind people. Everybody in town knew them and treated them with great affection. Yetta was no great driver, and I remember how she'd have tremendous difficulty parking. Whenever she went shopping downtown, she'd leave her car double-parked with the keys in the ignition. A policeman would come along, recognize the car, and park it for her. Then, when she was finished shopping, she'd find the right policeman and ask him where her car was. He'd give her back her keys, and point her in the right direction. Davenport was still that kind of place.

On Tuesday, June 7, 1966, Yetta died in St. Luke's Hospital after a three-year illness. She was only 62 years old.

Afterwards, Frank became less and less engaged in his company. It was partly deliberate, to give us up-and-coming managers our freedom. It was also a result of the growth and diversification of the business. There had been a time when Frank knew everyone in the company and their families as well. That had changed. We now had hundreds of people, and some of them did not stay at Alter for very long. I remember he once came across a young woman crying in the hallway. He didn't recognize her, nor she him. Seeking to comfort her, he went up to her and asked if there was anything he could do to help.

Frank and Yetta Alter in 1963.

"I've just been fired by Mr. Daniel," she sobbed. Harold Daniel was then our treasurer, having replaced George Otte.

"I'm sorry," said Frank, leaving in a hurry. "I wish I could do something, but I'm only the janitor here."

Frank married Belle Weissman, a girl he had met in school. They went to Las Vegas on their honeymoon, but when they arrived there, Frank suffered a heart attack. He was in the hospital for three weeks. The marriage didn't last, and they were soon divorced. Frank was very easy about the settlement. The only thing Frank insisted upon was that Belle should stop using the Alter name.

Over the following few years, I bought the rest of Frank's stake in Alter. I paid full price for it, because Arant and his lawyers may have been watching. Frank kept coming to company lunches until the end, and he'd sit in Chuck's office and listen to the trading. He kept himself well informed, and he still commanded an extraordinary loyalty among the people who had been at Alter for years. They'd do anything for him, as I would, mostly because they knew it was reciprocal, and that he would do everything he could for them.

They were his family.

On July 2, 1973, Frank came in to work as he often did, chatting with old friends, listening to the trading. Renee and I were at Disney World at the time with our younger children, Kathy and Rich. After work, Frank drove to our house to pick up Jeff and Rob to go out to dinner. On his way past the waterworks on River Drive, he had a car accident. He drove on to our house, but was feeling poorly. He came in and lay down. He said that the girls in the other car in the accident had been very rude to him. He was very upset. Jeff and Rob were so worried that they called an ambulance, but Frank grew increasingly ill. He suffered a heart attack. The ambulance driver told Rob and Jeff that they couldn't help at the hospital, so they stayed at our house and called Renee and me at Disney World. The next day, Frank died.

CHAPTER TEN
RIVER EXPANSION

It took us three years, but in 1963 Gordon Jones and I finally realized that there was a lot more corn and soybeans in Iowa than there was scrap iron! Until then, we'd limited ourselves to pushing scrap downstream and coal up, but those commodities were dwarfed by the potential downstream grain business.

We weren't the only people to discover this self-evident truth. The large grain dealers like Cargill, Bunge, and Archer-Daniels-Midland were building huge grain elevators on the Mississippi River and were starting to push vast quantities of grain down to New Orleans for export. As a result, there was plenty of business going, but winning it wasn't easy. For one thing, grain could not tolerate moisture, so we needed covered barges. Unfortunately, none of our barges had covers. We tried covering our open-hopper barges with canvas, but the grain companies wouldn't risk getting

Loading grain into covered barges in 1967.

In 1963, Alter barges began moving midwestern grain and soybeans down the Mississippi River.

moisture in their grain. We then tried to buy some used covered barges, but no one was selling. Finally, Gordon Jones and I won contracts from Pillsbury Grain and from Kent in Muscatine. On the strength of those contracts, we borrowed enough from Central Life Assurance of Des Moines to commission some new barges from Dravo.

Our timing couldn't have been better. It was boom times in river traffic. From the mid-1960s through the early 1970s, grain transportation on the Mississippi River grew 30 percent annually—and that despite the oil crisis, which saw the price of #2 diesel rise from 10 cents a gallon to 90 cents a gallon by 1979. We were soon doing such strong grain business around New Orleans that scheduling maximum work for our barges became a real challenge. We depended heavily on the "switch boats" that coupled and uncoupled barges, and then parked them in huge parking lots, called fleets, where they waited for more work. The trouble was, as barge traffic boomed, the switch boats became so busy around New Orleans, and the fleets so full, that we couldn't rely on them any more.

In 1964, we leased a mile of riverfront property eighteen miles upstream of New Orleans. We then chartered some switch boats and started Alter Fleet. Soon, other barge lines were using our services, so we doubled our property, adding a cleaning service, a dry dock, and a repair and maintenance service. In 1976, we wanted to change the company name, but we didn't want to repaint the boats (which wore our logo—a big "A" with an arrow), so we renamed it Azalea Fleet, after the beautiful local flower.

Barges parked at Azalea Fleet, north of New Orleans.

With more and more grain companies using barges to transport corn and soybeans down to New Orleans for export, there was more than enough downriver work to keep everyone busy. But the secret to consistently good profits was upriver business, and those payloads proved harder to find. Then one day Tom Belmar, our scrap traffic manager, heard that Sinclair Petrochemical was looking for a place to build a new fertilizer plant, and they needed a site with access to huge volumes of natural gas and phosphate rock. We helped them find a property near Fort Madison, Iowa, close by a natural gas pipeline and on the Mississippi River.

Now we just needed to find a way to move hundreds of thousands of tons of phosphate rock from Florida to Fort Madison. We approached Gulf Coast Transit, who shuttled barges between Tampa and Louisiana, and they agreed to bring the rock from Florida to New Orleans, where it was transferred to Alter barges. Overnight, we had all the upstream traffic we could handle—and a tremendous competitive advantage.

I I

As we added more and more barges, we also bought some small boats to push them around the Upper Mississippi. Mostly, we named the boats after members of the Alter family, and soon our fleet included the first M/V *Frank R. Alter* (1960), the M/V *Colonel Davenport* (1962), the M/V *Yetta Alter* (1963), the M/V *Renee G.* (1965), the first M/V *Phyllis* and the M/V *Fair Lady* (both 1966), and the first M/V *Beverly Ann* (1967).

In 1973, we added the second *Phyllis* and the *Miss Kathy*, Alter's first brand-new towboat. We held the dedication ceremony for both boats at the country club in Fort Madison, on top of the bluff high above the Mississippi River. The morning was cold and miserable, with heavy, drizzling skies, but just as we were about to begin the ceremony, a first wand of sunshine broke through the gray ceiling and magically turned the afternoon into a dazzling success. The *Phyllis* even did a little dance on the river. Frank gave a great speech, I remember, reminiscing about his early days in the scrap yard; he talked about how, as a young teenager, he'd gone out collecting scrap on his horse and wagon, and so he guessed he'd always been in the transport business. It made me realize just how far he'd come from his childhood in Russia.

Our crews worked a square watch, in shifts of six hours, seven days a week, for thirty days on, thirty days off. They typically consisted of a captain, a pilot, an engineer, an assistant engineer, a mate, four deckhands, and a cook. At Alter, we liked a female cook when possible. That way, the men shaved regularly and were better groomed.

Our small boats were fine for the Upper Mississippi, particularly around Davenport and Muscatine, where the locks and dams limited the number of barges any boat could push. Besides, the big towboat companies had largely overlooked the middle stretch of the Upper Mississippi. They all cherished the long-haul, from

The second Phyllis, named for Gordon Jones' wife, was dedicated at a ceremony in Fort Madison in 1973.

St. Louis to Minneapolis. At Alter Company, we were very happy with shorter trips. Our smaller horsepower boats enabled us to provide high-frequency, high-quality service to cities such as Dubuque, Muscatine, Keokuk, Clinton, and Quincy. We also offered towing to other barge lines, including competitors, which enabled us to achieve good turnaround on our equipment.

But on the Lower Mississippi, where big horsepower boats could comfortably push thirty or thirty-five barges at a time, our fleet was hopelessly underpowered. We considered buying some big boats, but they were very expensive. Instead, we adopted a different strategy. Most of our early competitors, like the Mechlings and the Roses, were born and bred on riverboats: their fathers piloting, their moms cooking. Many still lived on board. As a result, boats were their lives as well as their businesses; barges were just a necessary extra. And that meant that there were too many boats on the river and not enough barges.

But Gordon Jones and I both knew that barges, not boats, were the key to growth. Barges carried the payload and earned the cash. If you controlled barges, you could always hire boat owners to push those barges around. And barges were cheaper and easier to finance, too. Our plan was simple: we'd win solid five-year contracts with coal or grain companies, then take those contracts to our bankers as security for buying more barges, while we'd either charter boats or pay others to move them on the Lower Mississippi. The strategy worked brilliantly, and within thirteen years we'd acquired 218 barges, built with steel rub strips around them for longer life.

Our borrowings grew huge. Our borrowings from Central Life became so large that Central Life brought in Modern Woodmen, Farm Bureau, and State Farm to share the load. The consortium caused us some problems, which taught me a valuable truth about life: whether a person is good or bad does not depend on their position in life, or their financial status or intelligence. There are good and bad people of all kinds. The most honorable groups of people I have come across are the scrap dealers and small farmers that we regularly deal with—people who work long, hard hours at a tough business to earn their livelihood, honor their commitments, and take care of their families.

And the least honorable? Our agreement with our lending institutions specified fixed-interest loans of 6.25 percent per annum, even when general interest rates were on the rise. The contract was very specific about what we could and could not do, and every so often we needed a temporary waiver to one of the covenants. It was standard practice, and the members of the consortium agreed that if we needed any such waivers, we should negotiate them with Central Life, and then at the end of each year they would all sign the necessary documentation. One year, our auditors advised us that they couldn't finish their audit because State Farm, in Bloomington, hadn't returned the signed waivers. I was curious, so I went to see the manager and asked him why he refused to sign.

"But I never agreed to sign," he replied.

"Central Life agreed on your behalf," I reminded him, "and you promised to honor Central Life's actions."

"That was my predecessor's agreement," he said, "and I don't feel obligated by it."

"But we need those waivers," I protested. "We're in the middle of an audit."

"I'll tell you what," he said. "I'll sign the waivers if you'll accept an interest rate rise from 6.25 percent to 9.5 percent." With our audit already running late, I had no choice but to agree. I felt as if I had been blackmailed or mugged. Give me the scrap dealer any day.

To be fair, our relationships with the other institutions were always very good. We developed a tremendous relationship with Bruno Valente of the Heritage Pullman Bank, one of the few banks prepared to finance barges, and D.T. Doan and Keith Gunzenhauser at Central Life and Gary Stoeffen and Dave Eldridge at Modern Woodmen all acted honorably and well to us. On this one occasion, when I complained to Central Life about the behavior of the State Farm manager, they sympathized with me and agreed that State Farm had acted horribly. They promised me they'd not include State Farm in any future loans. However, they added, it was impossible for them to increase the interest rate for one partner without increasing it for every partner, so in that instance they got their 9.5 percent as well!

Our barge-buying strategy had one more drawback. It left us very dependent on the big boat owners of the Lower Mississippi. We got a commitment from Earl and Joe Rose, of the Rose Barge Line, to push our barges on the Lower Mississippi. The Roses did fine by us for a long time, and we renewed our contract with them year after year until renewal grew automatic. Or at least *almost* automatic. One year, a few weeks before our contract expired, Earl shuffled into our offices and told Gordon and me, apologetically, that he wouldn't be renewing next year. He muttered something about someone buying his company, needing his boats elsewhere, and not having spare capacity. I never did quite understand what he was trying to say, but I understood exactly what it meant. Gordon and I looked at each other in shock. Without big boats to push them, our barges were useless.

We spent two frantic weeks on the telephone, begging and borrowing enough pushing power to see us through the crisis. We made it, barely, but we knew we could never let ourselves be so exposed again. Our strategy had to change. We needed some big boats of our own. And that meant, somehow, we had to find some major financing.

III

I had heard, vaguely, of Title XI. It was a Maritime Administration scheme to encourage new shipbuilding, in an attempt to breathe some life back into the United States Merchant Marine. Thinking it might help our own boat-building problem, I went to Washington, D.C., for a meeting with four of the Administration's top people. I asked them if Title XI applied only to oceangoing vessels, or whether it covered boats on the Mississippi River.

"What business are you in exactly, young man?" asked one of them.

"We transport grain from Iowa and Illinois to the Gulf of Mexico," I replied.

"So why do you need boats?" asked a second man.

"Because," I explained, "we barge the grain on the Mississippi River."

"But," asked the third, "how do you get the grain from Iowa to the Mississippi?"

"Iowa borders the Mississippi," I told them. "The Mississippi divides Iowa from Illinois."

There was a moment of silence, while they digested this astonishing information. "I knew it was at St. Louis," muttered one. "I've been there."

"But wouldn't it be easier for you to go through Duluth and the Great Lakes?" asked another.

I left that meeting scratching my head in disbelief, appalled that the Maritime Administration could be so ignorant about America's inland waterways system. But their ignorance, to be fair, didn't last long. Within two years, they had extended their financing to new boat-building for the inland waterways system, guaranteeing 75 to 87.5 percent of loans, amortized over twenty-five years. In addition, a new IRS investment tax credit could almost entirely offset down payments. At Alter, we were always aggressive with taxes, using every method legitimately available to us to grow quickly. With the invaluable help of lawyers and accountants like Don Sitz of Lane & Waterman and

In 1974, Alter acquired the Beverly Ann, named for Chuck Smith's wife, and the Bernard G.
These big boats were designed for the Lower Mississippi.

Dave Wentworth and Don Decker of McGladrey, we leveraged tax incentives like Title XI for all they were worth. And that meant, at last, that we could afford some big boats.

In 1974, we added the second *Beverly Ann* and the *Bernard G.*, both for the Lower Mississippi. In 1977, we added the second *Frank R. Alter*, a 7,200 horsepower boat that could push thirty barges or more. It was a bittersweet moment for me, because it replaced the original M/V *Frank R. Alter*, the boat that had taken

At 7,200 horsepower, the second Frank R. Alter
is the largest boat in the Alter fleet.

us into the river transport business. The first *Frank* had always been one of my favorites, and it proved one of my best-ever investments, too. I'd paid just $125,000 for it in 1960 and spent $80,000 repowering it. We'd worked it hard for seventeen years, and still we sold it for more than $300,000—demonstrating the power of inflation. Remarkably, *Frank* is still going strong. Just a few months ago, it was sold to a South American company, and it is now hard at work on the Orinoco River.

I V

Not everyone was as happy as we were with the boom in the boat, barge, and grain business. The local railroads, traditionally the vehicle for Midwest grain to reach the coast, were devastated. Grain elevators by railroad tracks just a few blocks from the Mississippi River were made obsolete almost overnight. But the railroads helped hurry their own downfall. They couldn't see that cooperative joint ventures with barge lines were their future, and so they refused to let their trains freight grain to riverside elevators. We had to truck it instead, which was far more expensive and meant that farmers, railroads, and barge companies were all losing out.

That seemed such a waste that I called on the president of the Milwaukee Railroad and suggested we form a partnership to rail grain to our docks, then barge it downriver. He refused, stating bluntly that he considered barges to be his mortal enemy and vowing he'd allow such a joint venture only over his dead body. His pronouncement proved more accurate than he would have wanted, because within a few years, he'd led Milwaukee Railroad into bankruptcy, and he was out of a job.

But Milwaukee Railroad didn't quite die. His successor, who led the railroad out of

*Colonel Lycan of the U.S. Army Corps of Engineers joined us in commemorating
the nation's first rail-barge joint bill of lading.*

bankruptcy, was happy to strike a deal, enabling the issue of joint rail-barge bills of
lading. In 1978, they railed a first joint shipment of grain to Davenport, where we
transferred it to our barges and pushed it down to New Orleans. As the first joint bill
of lading citing a railroad and a barge line, it gained considerable publicity and gave
us another edge on our competition. The partnership worked out fine for Milwaukee
Railroad, too, and "ping-ponging" grain-filled cars proved efficient and profitable
for them.

Our truck fleet was doing well, too, fueled by the growth of our scrap yards and
our barge business. We were collecting and delivering scrap from the hundred-mile
area around Davenport, and we'd also built up a solid business back hauling salt,
grain, and other commodities. Encouraged, we bought several big rigs to take goods to
California, Texas, and other long-haul destinations, and won ICC interstate licenses.

Like all young businesses, it needed someone to take charge of it and drive it
on to success, but that never
happened. Even in the good
times, our trucks didn't
make much money. Then the
industry was deregulated and
profits tumbled everywhere.
Prospects for recovery looked
so bleak, we cut back Alter's
truck operations to salt, grain,
and scrap.

*Alter Trucking & Terminal grew because of our successful
scrap business and the barge line.*

CHAPTER ELEVEN
REGULATION AND SHREDDERS

In the early 1970s, in an effort to curb inflation, the Nixon Administration introduced price controls. The controls did little to stop rising prices, but they did manage to do our scrap business a whole heap of harm, because while most dealers ignored the controls completely, we actually respected them. As a result, our bids for scrap quickly became uncompetitive, and we survived only by hiring lawyers to find a way through the labyrinth of legislation. If anything positive came from that experience, it was that we learned how the federal government thought. It was like a vast, blind elephant crashing wildly through the jungle. If you could stand behind the elephant, then it would clear your path for you, and life was easy. *But if you stood in its way...!*

This was particularly true of environmental legislation. Much of the legislation was good and timely. It helped clean up polluted streams and rivers, for example, many of which had become horrible. But other legislation was simply counterproductive. For some reason, environmentalists seemed to dislike scrap dealers, as if we caused waste and pollution rather than cured it. Perhaps they didn't realize that people like us pioneered recycling thousands of years ago, or that the scrap industry was the world's most efficient recycling machine. Or if they were aware, they certainly didn't seem to accept that scrap dealers needed to make profits to survive. Take away profit, and you kill recycling. Yet time and time again, that is what environmentalists tried to do.

The many millions of cars in America, for example, needed hundreds of millions of car batteries. As those batteries died each year, the scrap industry collected them and sold them to lead smelters who melted out the lead and supplied it back to battery makers and other users. It was a classic production cycle that cut down on lead mining at the same time it solved the problem of what to do with the poisonous dead batteries. Then the environmentalists decided to get involved. They introduced complex rules and regulations on lead-handling and took all the profit out of the business. Naturally, many scrap dealers refused to handle dead batteries any more, so they piled up at gas stations and auto wrecker yards. But the auto wreckers and garage owners knew the batteries were a potential EPA liability, so many of them waited till nightfall, threw them in their pickup trucks, and dumped them in ditches and woods all around the country, where they leaked their contamination into the very streams and rivers the EPA was trying to clean. The unprecedented pollution that followed was the EPA's fault. They should have thought through their idea before they made it law.

There was worse. The fundamental regulations on scrap were not drafted carefully. Scrap, although a recyclable, was considered a waste product. That meant that every scrap dealer was a potentially responsible party (PRP) at Superfund site cleanups. Some battery manufacturers and lead reclaimers had had lousy environmental controls, and were declared Superfund sites. Now, all the scrap dealers who ever sold them batteries were liable for the cleanup. The policy was implemented viciously. There were cases where we didn't even sell a particular company lead but were still pressured for a contribution. Sometimes we were told that for $2,000, we'd be let off the hook. Put simply, it was blackmail, and still is, but until the law gets changed, it is legal.

That wasn't the only trouble with the environmental movement. One company wanted to put a plant into Muscatine, Iowa, but the environmentalists were terrified that it would jeopardize the future of the Illinois Spotted Mussel or some such "endangered" species. As a result, the plant wasn't built, and the potential new jobs were lost. Later, it was found that the mussels lived happily in Texas, Arkansas, Tennessee, and all over the country. When the EPA was asked why they'd put the mussel on the endangered species list, they replied they didn't know there were any others and didn't have the money to go look. The same happened with snail darters and wetlands. Sadly, our politicians were too frightened of the environmental vote to stand up for industry. One local representative agreed wholeheartedly with me on the issue, but whenever he voted in Congress, he voted with the environmental lobby. I asked him why and he told me bluntly that there were many more environmentalists voting than there were industrialists.

The environmentalists also came after car burning. It was common practice in scrap yards to pour kerosene on car hulks, then throw a match on them to burn off all the upholstery and other "fluff" before they were baled. To be fair, it wasn't a clean process, but instead of helping find alternatives or gradually cutting it over many years, the EPA simply banned it. The legislation was a disaster and put hundreds of people out of work. It also meant that cars were uneconomic to recycle. At once, abandoned car hulks began piling up in streets, parking lots, and ravines all over America. Incidentally, the laws didn't even make the air cleaner; they only made it look cleaner. Often, controlled "clean" emissions were more harmful than the dirty smoke had been.

Meanwhile, the cost of complying with the new clean air regulations was greater than many foundries were worth, and they were simply put out of business. As a result, our castings industry collapsed. America's tank manufacturers began buying tank turrets from Germany, and airframe companies started subcontracting Japanese companies to build components for our fighter planes. Can you imagine another war, with us depending on Germany for tanks and Japan for fighter planes? The single regulation banning car burning therefore led to terrible pollution, waste, a weakening of our national defense, *and* the loss of thousands of American jobs. And in its place we saw billions of dollars going overseas.

It also led to rampant inflation. Our nation's best brains in Washington and New York were scratching their heads, trying to figure out why inflation was so bad. If they'd come to the rust belt, I'd have showed them. Complying with environmental legislation was doubling the cost of basic raw materials like steel and lead. It didn't take a genius to see how that would feed inflation. But of course no economists or politicians ever came out to the rust belt. Instead, Paul Volcker at the Federal Reserve Board pushed interest rates up to 20 percent. He killed inflation all right, but only because he killed industry first. To this day, there is nothing in the textbooks about how environmental legislation caused inflation.

Another government mistake was to finance Social Security out of payroll taxes. Because overseas manufacturers were not obliged to pay U.S. Social Security taxes when they sold goods here, that gave them a terrific advantage. It would have been simple enough to finance Social Security through a sales tax, or a value-added tax, so that all manufacturers selling goods in America would have to share the burden. That would help put our system back on its feet.

I I

Whatever the rights and wrongs of the ban on car burning, we had to find some way to deal with it and still make money. At Davenport, we experimented with a car-burning incinerator fitted with an afterburner to burn up the smoke, making it invisible and legal, but the incinerator only incinerated itself. Then we heard rumors that Proler, of Texas, was making clean steel scrap out of automobiles without burning them. No one knew how. They'd soon set up a second site at Kansas City, a third in Chicago, then a fourth in London, England. Finally, we discovered that they'd built a huge hammermill, or shredder, that could smash cars into small chunks, like a sink disposal unit. They then used magnets and huge filters to separate the ferrous metal from the fluff. If they could do it, we decided, so could we.

We commissioned Hammermills Inc., a Cedar Rapids manufacturer of rock crushers, to build us a hammermill. But their first effort threw chunks of car all over our Davenport yard; and when a John Deere buyer looked at the scrap for quality, he gave it the thumbs-down. Next, we heard about a man named Roy Eidal, from Albuquerque, New Mexico. Eidal supplied trailers to the Middle East to ferry oil rigs across the desert, but he had also designed a shredder, rumored to make beautifully clean and dense scrap. I went to see him in 1968 and found that the rumors were true. It was a vertical shaft machine that shredded cars into scrap of such fine quality that I offered to start a joint venture with him.

Eidal machines produced wonderfully dense scrap, but they broke down too often to make them marketable.

We branded the scrap "Puremelt", and set up Eidal shredders in sites from Fort Lauderdale, Florida, to Mobile, Alabama. It was a great scheme, but it had one flaw. The Eidal machines lived up to the sound of their name—they were constantly idle. They broke down every few hours. Even Jake Barnes, as good with machinery as anyone I've met, had problems keeping the Council Bluffs machine going. Roy Eidal worked hard to fix the problem but never succeeded. Eventually, running out of cash, he merged with a competitor. Arabian arms dealer Adnan Kashoggi was one of the new company's leading customers and a major shareholder, and he was worried that I was a Zionist, so our partnership came to an end. It was just as well: Eidal machines never did work for us.

After Eidal, we worked with Dravo on a similar vertical shaft hammermill, but even though it was much heavier and sturdier than Eidal's machine, it also broke too often. We brought a lawsuit against Dravo, and Dravo made a counterclaim, which (because it was unfounded) didn't worry me. I should have known better. Thanks to the imaginative storytelling of several of their employees on the witness stand, we were held liable for $1 million. It was an expensive way to learn that there is no right and wrong in court, just winners and losers. I learned something else, too. Bill Johnson, our attorney with Lord, Bissell, & Brook, got it right when he advised me to stay away from the cutting edge of technology in the future and let other people do the experimenting. Starting a whole new venture can be a very costly education—a lot more costly than going to Harvard or Yale. But to be fair, as I later found out with riverboat gambling, as long as you analyze new projects very carefully, as long as you leave yourself a sufficient margin of error for whatever might go wrong (and something unexpected *always* goes wrong), and as long as you ask yourself "why," as well as "why not," new projects are often very well worth the effort and risk in the long run.

But we still had to do something to recycle cars. So many abandoned car hulks now littered the streets that the State of Iowa begged us to put in any kind of reliable shredder. To solve the problem we looked at some Newell machines. Newell made horizontal feed shredders, which made lighter scrap than the vertical shaft machines of Eidal and Dravo, but their quality was fine for electric furnaces. They cost $2 million apiece, and they churned thirty car bodies in an hour. Most important, they were reliable. In 1975, we bought one for Davenport and one for Council Bluffs.

III

Our efforts to lead the field in the shredder revolution taught me a great deal about the way industry evolves. Every so often, something new comes along. Someone invents something revolutionary, or government alters a policy, or the economy shifts, and an entire industry is created or suddenly and completely transformed. It is like a huge wave, washing away the old, bringing in the new. Anyone in the right place at the right time, who sees the wave early enough, can ride it on to success. Miss the wave and you drown. At Alter, we knew heavy equipment would be necessary for success in the scrap yard, and our instinct and vision had served us well in the barge business. I thought we'd also caught the wave with Eidal, but here our technology let us down.

In garbage processing, Alter almost caught another wave. As had happened with car burning, the burning of waste in wire baskets and incinerators was banned. As a result, dumps were soon replaced by landfill sites. Landfills were very different from dumps. For a start, they needed special containers and container trucks, which were almost identical to those already used by scrap yards. We decided to get involved. We started selling garbage compactors, and our trucks began picking up garbage all over the Midwest, from the Twin Cities to Des Moines. Eagle Foods was one of our biggest customers, and we served them not only in the Quad Cities but also in Chicago.

We never made any money, though. Our manager was a terrific salesman, but he was less skilled at operations. He never could supervise our truck drivers properly. Every other day, it seemed, one of them was getting stuck in a soft spot at a landfill or falling over. It happened so often I considered putting roll bars on our trucks! As ever, a time came when Alter needed cash desperately. We studied our businesses hard, to determine what was important to our future and what could go. We decided that the garbage business was least important and could be sold.

Our manager got in touch with Browning Ferris Industries (BFI), and they sent down a vice president to Davenport, who negotiated a very nice deal for his company, buying our garbage business for about $500,000 in cash. After negotiating for two days, I thought we had a deal, and as we shook hands, I asked him if the deal was final.

"Well," he shrugged, "it's final, subject to the approval of my bosses."

"And how long will that take?"

"Three, four days."

"Fine," I told him, "but you realize it won't be final on our side either, until you get the approval."

He agreed with that, but on the way to the airport, he made a bad mistake. He boasted to our manager that he *did* have the authority to make a firm commitment, but he hadn't done so because he wanted to let me hang for a couple of days. I wasn't having that, so I called Jim Watts, a garbage hauler from Rock Island, and he put me in touch with Waste Management in Oakbrook, Illinois. When I'd told him about our business, they offered me $100,000 more than BFI had. They also promised that I'd have the check first thing in the morning.

The moment the check arrived, I sent a telegram to BFI terminating our negotiations and advising them that we'd just sold to someone else. They called at once, furious, insisting that they had a deal. But they hadn't, and I had 100,000 reasons to be happy they had "let me hang" for a couple of days. I still don't quite know what their negotiator hoped to achieve by making me wait. Many people hesitate to make tough decisions because they're frightened of making mistakes. But often, the biggest mistake is to hesitate. Frank Alter was always smart enough to accept it when his people made mistakes. He used to say that the only people who never made mistakes were the people who didn't do anything. Over the years, he has been proven right. But that didn't mean that Frank was soft. If you made the same mistake *twice...!*

I V

Environmental regulation was tough on big scrap yards and small ones, but it was particularly brutal for mid-sized yards. Too large to fill a small niche in the market, and too small to be able to afford all the new and hugely expensive machines, they were simply squeezed out of business. At Alter, we devised a two-tier yard system to deal with this problem. We equipped our large, regional yards (Davenport, St. Paul, and Council Bluffs) with the finest available heavy machinery, then surrounded them with smaller feeder yards, equipped with no more than a scale, a portable car crusher, one or two cranes, and as many trucks as they needed.

By the 1960s, Alter was one of only two sizable scrap dealers left in the Quad Cities. The other was Midland Iron & Steel, the major supplier of International Harvester's Farmall plant in Rock Island. Midland was run by Al Livingston, and he and Frank didn't like each other at all. Their rivalry was known all around town. Al would bid up prices just to rile Frank, commenting he'd rather give the money to "Uncle Sam" than let Frank get it, and I'm sure Frank would do the same to Al when he had the chance. All in all, the competition wasn't helpful to either side.

Al died in 1966, and his estate didn't specify who should take over the yard. He had no children, but two of his nephews, Frank Wallace and Hank Davis, worked for him. Both were talented, but their differing business styles caused friction between them. Both wanted to buy the yard from the estate, but Hank Davis finally succeeded. He did a great job with Midland, too, and later sold half to us. At that time, we both notified our major customers of the deal and promised that our investment would not impact Alter's competitiveness with Midland. When Hank's sons Mitch and Marty took over, they expanded into scrap paper, wooden pallet grinding, and other ventures. As we'd promised our customers, we kept competing hard with Midland.

We acquired some other yards, too. In 1977, we bought David Solomon's Dubuque yard. David was in his seventies by then and wanted to slow down. His only stipulation to the sale was that he be allowed to keep his office at the yard so that he could come in every day and read the *Wall Street Journal*. I suspect he just wanted some quiet time away from Mrs. Solomon (who used to grab my arm during the negotiations and tell me I didn't realize what a wonderful deal I was getting), but whatever the motivation, it was a pleasure to buy him out. He kept a good yard, was a great personality, and did everything he could to make the transition painless, both for us and for his customers. He took my son Jeff out to meet all his major clients, and during the meeting he'd take the client's hand and look earnestly into his eyes. "Paul," he'd say. "It's all right. These Goldsteins are good people, they'll take care of you."

We also tried to acquire Joe Blumenthal's yard in Des Moines. We thought the deal was settled and were about to sign when he told us he'd sold to Ben Schwartz, a scrap dealer and speculator from Marshalltown, Iowa. Instead, we set up shop in a Des Moines gas station, then bought a property on Maury Street and fitted it with two trucks and a car crusher. A year later, we bid for Joe Cohen's yard in Cedar Rapids. When we turned up to finalize the negotiations, however, Joe told us he'd just sold to Ben Schwartz. Ben was becoming a problem. We knew he didn't much like us. Chuck Smith had called on him years earlier, and when Chuck handed Ben his card, Ben took one look at it and put it in his ashtray.

"So you're with Frank Alter," said Ben, stubbing his cigar out on it. "Thanks for visiting."

"My pleasure," answered Chuck. "Come up to Davenport some time, and we'll return every bit of your hospitality."

Ironically, when Frank Alter married Belle Weissman after Yetta died, his new wife was Ben Schwartz's mother-in-law. For a while that made me Ben's brother-in-law! Fortunately, that didn't last. We never did make friends with Ben, but we eventually got our yards. Ben lost many millions speculating on copper in the 1980s, and his sons Paul and Harry, both good guys, sold us the two yards we thought we'd bought years earlier.

Lois Hansen, my personal secretary for many years.

By now, Alter had interests and business all over the country, and I was traveling so much I barely knew what day of the week it was or which town I was in. I'd never much taken to the idea of having a secretary, but with so much going on, I was finally persuaded it was necessary. The first few secretaries I had, however, only strengthened my feelings against them. One time, I was taking Renee and our four kids to Disney World and asked my secretary to order me a rental car big enough to take six people.

"What if they don't have any big cars left?" she asked, as I was on my way out the door.

"Then get me two small ones," I joked. Of course, when I arrived in Orlando, Avis had two little compacts waiting for me!

I was beginning to despair of ever finding a good secretary. We seemed to be running a new advertisement every month. Then Art Petersen suggested I interview Lois Hansen. Art had worked with Lois at Nichol's Homeshield and thought she'd do a fine job. She came in for an interview, and we got on brilliantly from the start.

It proved to be the perfect match, and she's been with me ever since. Thankfully, between them, Lois and Renee have kept me pointed in the right direction over the past few years, always telling me where to go, and when to go. Lois, in fact, proved so valuable that we appointed her the first woman officer of Alter Company (aside from my wife). Now, of course, I wouldn't know what to do without good secretaries, so I'd like to add a word of thanks for the tremendous work Rose Hayes has done for me in Casino America's Boca Raton office, and also to Joyce Hart in Biloxi.

V

While we were building our iron and steel business, extending our yard network, and acquiring new machinery, we were also working hard on rebuilding our nonferrous business, much of which we'd lost in the Alter-Alloy split. Nonferrous was (and is) very different from ferrous. Chemistry control and grading are of paramount importance, and quantities are much smaller. Where steel and iron are priced by the ton, copper and aluminum are so much more valuable that they are priced by the pound. As a result, freight costs make up a smaller proportion of total price, which allows greater purchase and sales range.

Back in 1960, we'd been selling battery lead to Schuykill Lead, a Baton Rouge company, who then refined it into ingots for tetraethyl gasoline. But Schuykill had a problem with Arant one time, and even after the split they wouldn't do business with us. I wanted to change their mind, so I went down to Baton Rouge with Don Geurink and called on them. The plant manager advised us that Reed Evans, the owner, wasn't feeling well that day and suggested we head up to his house. We were shown into a living room with a picture window looking out onto the backyard, and we sat down to wait.

Suddenly, there was the loudest roar I'd ever heard. Don and I jumped out of our skins. We turned around and saw a full-grown lion, with its paws up on the other side of the picture window, and it had seen us. As we ran for the door, it opened, and Reed Evans came in. "Don't be scared," he said. "He wouldn't hurt a fly." It wasn't the health of the flies Don and I were worried about, but we figured our host knew more about the lion's appetites then we did, so we sat down, hammered out our case, and thought (mistakenly) we had won ourselves some business. But we weren't through with our shocks just yet. When I later visited a scrap dealer in New Orleans, he confided that until a recent operation, Mr. Evans' first name had been Rita.

CHAPTER TWELVE
THE 1980s

The Quad Cities is a wonderful place to live, but for a barge line it has one major disadvantage. Every winter, the Arctic weather turns Old Man River into a giant ice-skating rink. The annual freeze stops barge transportation on the Upper Mississippi for up to four months, affects America's internal and external trading, and (not least important to me) reduces our profitability. What makes it so frustrating is that there is no need for the ice to stop traffic, at least in our area. The Canadians operate icebreakers on the Saint Lawrence Seaway, while our own government uses icebreakers on the polar ice caps. Surely an icebreaker made sense for the Upper Mississippi. After all, America's inland waterways system is one of our most efficient methods of transport.

Ice on the Upper Mississippi.

I was not alone in believing that a government-sponsored icebreaker was a good idea for the Upper Mississippi, and I became a strong and public advocate of the plan. Lash barges had just been invented, I remember. Lash barges (an acronym for "Light Aboard Ship") were 300-ton barges invented by naval architect Jerry Goldman. They could be pushed down to New Orleans as normal, then loaded fully laden onto a mother ship. The mother ship would then sail across the Atlantic and release the barges, still loaded, into Europe's inland waterways system, or wherever. They were a huge advance in containerization, massively reducing loading and unloading time, and they were launched with a big splash by Spiro Skouros, head of Presidential Line, at a Mississippi Valley Association meeting in Davenport's Blackhawk Hotel.

It was a major event. The U.S. Secretary of Transportation was there, so I used my place on the speaker's roster to speak out for an icebreaker on the Upper Mississippi, arguing that if we could put a man on the moon, we could surely get a barge to Dubuque in winter. It was a good speech, but the Sierra Club and the Izaac Walton League, both lavishly supported by the railroads, said that the Mississippi freeze was one of the great and immutable laws of nature, and breaking the ice would be somehow catastrophic. We never did get our icebreaker, even though a study by the U.S. Army Corps of Engineers supported my position that one was both feasible and

Renee and I meet Jimmy and Rosalynn Carter at Davenport.

economic, at least as far as Dubuque. Instead, we tried our best to extend the barging season any way we could. An Alter barge was invariably first in to Davenport in the spring, and we were the last to retreat when winter began to close in. Our boats battled ice jams even when good sense should have dictated a safer course, but at least our courage (if that's what it's called) made us popular with our customers.

Ironically, the only winter so mild that the Upper Mississippi didn't freeze was the winter of 1979. When December was through and the river still open, I had visions of loading barges all year round. But then the Soviet Union invaded Afghanistan, and President Jimmy Carter, in a desperate effort not to look weak, banned exports of grain to the USSR. Russia was by far the largest buyer of our grain at the time, and the embargo devastated the Midwest farming industry. We didn't load another barge that winter, even though the river stayed open; and for the following thirteen years, the terrible effects of the embargo were felt throughout Iowa and Illinois. Though Carter claimed to be aiming at the Russians, it was us he hit.

Incidentally, President Carter had one opportunity to help our towboat fortunes, but it came to nothing. One time, we heard that Carter and his family were coming down the Mississippi River on the *Delta Queen*. They were stopping at Davenport for a reception given by Mary Ellen Chamberlain. I was one of the locals who lined up as the *Delta Queen* was docking, and when the motorcade dropped off President Carter, his wife Rosalynn and daughter Amy, and Senator and Mrs. John Culver, I took my opportunity to speak to him.

"Mr. President," I said, "I'm glad to see that you're on the Mississippi River. I'm in the towboat business. We have a major problem, and you could really help us. There is a real bottleneck at lock and dam 26 at Alton, Illinois, and our boats and barges have to wait three or four days to get through. If you could lend us your support, I'm sure we could do something about it. If you'd like to get off the *Delta Queen* and travel on a towboat for a few days, please let me know."

President Carter turned to his wife. "Would you like to do that, Rosalynn?"

"Huh?"

"Would you like to get on a towboat for a while?" But Rosalynn made the worst face you could possibly imagine, puckering up like a prune. I got the message.

"Mr. President," I said, "I'll leave my card with your security people in case you change your mind." He never did, of course.

Carter's grain embargo was a sign of bad things to come. The inland waterways system had enjoyed a long boom, and now, inexorably, it moved on to bust. For us, it started, ironically, with a Fiasco. After the Eidal machines had lived up to their name by invariably being idle, I should have slammed down the phone when a Mr. Fiasco called, but I didn't. He wanted us to commit to charter thirty barges that a New York investor named Bob Gibbs had under construction. He offered a good rate, so we agreed. Then, a while later, Gibbs asked if we could lend him $4 million over ninety days. Harold Daniel, our treasurer, scraped together the money, taking the barges as security. The ninety days stretched out longer and longer. Fiasco was living up to his name. Our $4 million was lost, and all we had to show for it was more barges and a significant debt to the Midlantic Bank of New Jersey. In the good times, Alter could have lived with one bad debt and a few more barges, but the times weren't good. They were turning bad. Very, very bad.

I felt it in my bones when a Merrill Lynch investment banker asked if I'd manage some barges for one of his funds. I told him no. But his request made me anxious about the future of barges. The Maritime Administration was still offering Title XI for investment in transport, and that, combined with the IRS investment tax credit, had led Wall Street bankers to invest in barges for their clients as tax shelters. We found ourselves competing with doctors from Florida and dentists from San Diego. That scared me. After all, I didn't head south to treat arthritis or fix people's teeth. Barges had been making money because there had been enough work to go around. Now, shipyards that had been building a few hundred barges a year suddenly started building thousands. With the grain embargo and the overexpansion of the barge fleet, work was drying up. Rates were already dropping, and a price war was surely coming. The time had come to quit.

First, I offered our barge interests to Jack Lambert of Twin City Barge Line. Then I heard that George Steinbrenner from American Shipbuilding was also interested. He sent over Ed Forbes, his president, to deal with me, and, thinking I was being clever, I stalled Lambert. It was the worst move I could have made. Even as I delayed, the bottom fell out of the barge industry, everyone started slashing rates, and we slumped into thirteen years of depression. The great irony was that the IRS later ruled that most investment in barges was not eligible for tax shelter status to the casual investor, and many of them were held liable for back taxes *and* for their losses. The whole boom and bust was unnecessary, and it was due to Wall Street bankers not knowing their own business, let alone ours. The damage to the barge line industry was awful. From good profitability and rapid expansion, we started losing money.

But still the bad news kept coming in.

One of our greatest competitive strengths had long been our connection with Sinclair Petrochemical's Fort Madison fertilizer plant, which gave our barges plenty of upriver traffic. Even when Sinclair sold the plant to Arco Chemical, who sold it on to First Mississippi, we still continued to supply it with phosphate rock. On the strength of that contract, we financed three new boats and many new barges. But then the fertilizer market itself turned into a heap of manure, and First Mississippi closed its plant and unilaterally canceled its barge contracts.

That was terrible news for us, but we hadn't been completely dumb. Aware how dependent we were on First Mississippi, we had written into our contracts that if they canceled, they'd still have to pay us a minimum fee. But First Mississippi refused to honor the contract, thereby forcing us to take them to court. Meantime, the payments on our barges and boats were bleeding us to death. Chuck cut wages at the scrap yards by 15 percent, and John McKenzie (who took over from Gordon Jones in 1982) cut wages at the barge company by 20 percent. Even so, we struggled to survive, especially when V.O. Figge, who had been our banker at Davenport Bank & Trust for decades, decided that he wanted my signature on all our company loans. At our worst moment, when we were studying our options, First Mississippi offered us a token quantity of cash as full settlement. Although it represented only a fraction of what they owed us, we were so desperate for funds we had to accept.

There was one final twist to the collapse of the barge industry. Alter was not publicly traded, its shares were closely held, and its profits were reinvested rather than paid out in dividends. There was no trading in company stock, so stock options and other share plans were pointless. On the other hand, we wanted to reward our people for their services and instill some pride of ownership.

The barges gave us a way to accomplish that. It worked like this: barges had been increasing in value since the 1950s, and the trend seemed set to continue. When we bought new barges, therefore, we provided finance to our key employees, enabling them to purchase shares in the barges. Then, when the original investment was paid back, they still owned the barges, which had usually gained in value. The plan became so successful that we extended it to everyone. The trouble was, just as we opened it up, the market collapsed. Barge values plummeted, and we had to buy out our employees so they didn't get hurt.

II

There's only one business that prospers in a deep recession, and that's the bankruptcy industry. As our barge profits sank, our scrap yards also found themselves in trouble. Farmers were hurting, and that meant that the Midwest's agricultural companies were closing their plants and laying off their people. As a result, many small businesses were going bust and leaving bad debts, which inevitably led to other bankruptcies. The pyramid built on itself.

I'd known for years how vulnerable scrap yards were to cash flow problems. We paid peddlers cash on delivery but billed our customers on terms of up to thirty days—and sometimes longer than that. I remember selling scrap to U.S. Steel and buying from them, too. We used to bill them net thirty days, while they'd billed us net ten. One time, their accounts receivable department sent us an angry telegram complaining we were ten days late with our payment. When we pointed out that they were sixty days overdue on their payment to us, they couldn't have cared less.

"Too bad," they said. "Receivables and payables have nothing to do with each other."

Then, when the huge Penn Central Railroad took bankruptcy, I realized that any size customer could go bankrupt, however good their reputation and their credit rating.

*Loading scrap for international sales. At the peak of our export business,
we averaged one cargo of 25–30,000 tons every month.*

I learned from that lesson and looked into credit insurance. It was so cheap, I decided to insure Alter against late payments and bad debts. As part of the service, our insurance company checked out and approved the financial strength and creditworthiness of each new customer, and that certainly helped us survive the domestic recession. As many steel mills went bankrupt in the 1980s, many of our scrap competitors who hadn't insured their accounts sank beneath their unbearable burden of bad debts.

Fortunately, even as the American scrap market collapsed, the international market remained robust. We hired East Coast consultants John Lehman and Irv Lichtenfeld to show us how to increase our "blue water" sales, exporting scrap across the Pacific and Atlantic Oceans and supplementing scrap from our own yards with purchases from all over the inland waterways system. We'd handle entire deals: negotiating sales direct with the overseas mills or their American buyers, buying the scrap, chartering the vessels, and arranging the stevedoring. We developed great relationships with mills in Korea and Turkey, and we also sold scrap to the People's Republic of China, Brazil, Venezuela, and India.

We even did two demolition deals, in which the vessels carrying the scrap were themselves part of the cargo; for one, we bought the *Gypsum Duchess*, a 10,000-ton gypsum self-loading vessel. We had to reflag it when we took ownership, so we had someone lean over the side with a spray-can and called it the *Duchess I*, then flagged it from Panama. We put on a Pakistani crew, loaded it with scrap, and sailed it down to Brazil where the cargo and vessel were both sold as scrap. Then we sent the crew home. The only surviving memento of the *Duchess* is the ship's wheel and compass that my son Rob has in his office.

Another time, we took an order for some 22,000 tons of scrap to be delivered to Hanbo Steel in the port of Inchon, Korea. We rounded up the scrap in some old lash barges. The barges were small, with single-skin sides and double-skin ends, and they each carried about 300 tons of cargo. We had to fill seventy-three of them with scrap from all over the Gulf Coast. Scrap is tough to load onto a lash barge, especially an old one. If you drop it in with cranes, it can easily puncture a hole in the thin skin. Keeping all these barges afloat while we accumulated them was quite a challenge, and all the way to New Orleans we pumped water to keep them afloat.

At the peak of our export brokerage business, we averaged one cargo of between 25,000 and 35,000 tons each month, and it constituted about 15 percent of all our scrap sales. It was sophisticated, exciting, and challenging, but it was no nine-to-five job. We'd load in the small hours of the morning, making sure that the captain didn't sail until he'd signed our documents. International negotiations were also often conducted at 3 a.m., when our customers were awake. Our brokers often had to drop everything to fly to New York to negotiate letters of credit, because with interest rates at 20 percent, every hour of a $5 million letter of credit cost money.

One time my son Rob was racing to the New Orleans airport to catch his plane, which was landing as he sped up the adjacent highway. He'd been up for twenty-four hours of tough work already and hadn't had the chance to clean up. He was so dirty, he says, he couldn't stand the way he smelled. When he got on the plane, he found himself in the seat next to Congressman Dick Gephardt. Thankfully, he didn't introduce himself.

But export, while profitable, didn't last long. A revolution was taking place in steel production, both in America and around the world. The first minimill had been built in Sterling, Illinois, in the 1940s, but it was not until the late 1970s that electric arc furnaces made a real dent in the dominance of traditional open-hearth steel mills. The revolution was hugely significant to scrap yards because minimills did not use iron ore and blast furnaces. They survived entirely on scrap, and their electric arc furnaces slashed production costs for quality bar, plate, beam, and coil steel by as much as $100 a ton.

Casting floor at Nucor Steel.

Now, with North America racing out of recession, minimills appeared everywhere. In our areas of operation, North Star Steel put one in St. Paul, Minnesota. Another went into Wilton, Iowa. In Canada, minimills went up in Edmonton, Calgary, Regina, and Winnipeg. Then Nucor built a minimill on the river at Blytheville, Arkansas. Where we'd been buying and exporting 30,000 tons a month, Nucor started buying 100,000 tons a month. Later, they added a second mill, and their monthly intake rose to 300,000 tons. They sucked in all the scrap from the inland waterways system like a huge vacuum cleaner and effectively ended our export business.

I I I

But our greatest problem in the scrap business was our New Orleans yard. In 1980, the European owners of Bayou Steel, a new riverfront minimill in La Place, Louisiana, approached us. They wanted to take advantage of the good freight rates on the river and asked us to broker and supply their scrap. We set up a brokerage office in Birmingham, Alabama, and also supplied them out of our own yards. The partnership worked well for a while. Everyone was happy.

Our first inkling of trouble came when Bayou Steel's melter declared he wanted only shredded scrap. The mill had previously agreed to take a certain percentage of baled cars, but no longer. They were good customers, however, and we wanted to accommodate them. Because we had no shredding facilities in the region, we began thinking about buying a scrap yard and shredder near the mill, duplicating our Council Bluffs situation.

In May 1981, Ed Levy, a New Orleans scrap dealer, passed away, and we bought his yard on the industrial canal. It was a bad mistake. The yard had terrible problems. It sat on such low ground that it was not so much on the canal as in it. When heavy rains came or a stiff wind pushed water in from the Gulf, it filled up like a bathtub, sometimes three or four feet deep. It was horrible to work in: our machinery kept breaking down, and our office had to be up on stilts. Setting up was a problem, too. Hiring good people was a nightmare. The yard was right by the housing projects, packed with chronic drug users and welfare recipients. Few of them were willing to work, and those who were kept wrecking our equipment and hurting themselves. We never did assemble a good team.

My son Jeff was in charge of the yard. His first job was getting rid of the large tonnage of scrap that we'd bought along with the yard, some of which had been there so long it had sprouted trees. We took aerial photographs to give ourselves an idea of how much scrap there was, but we could never get our inventory to balance for long. We quickly learned why Ed Levy had been a speculator, not a processor: processing scrap in that yard was a nightmare. The yard's shear was so far from the river it was hopeless for loading barges. We knew we had to move it, but setting anything heavy near the riverbank was like trying to build a skyscraper on a bowl of thick soup. Instead, we put it on a monster barge. This unique feat of engineering made it transportable along the Mississippi. Alas, it never worked consistently.

With all of its problems, the New Orleans yard wasn't producing enough scrap, so we bought a small feeder yard in Baton Rouge and hired a manager who talked a great story. He could have talked a cat off a shrimp boat. But the guy wouldn't do his job, and so that turned into a whole other farce. As if all that wasn't enough, our competition created even more problems. The Diefenthals were New Orleans' leading scrap merchants, and they did all kinds of things to persuade us to leave. Jeff shuttled between Davenport and Louisiana trying everything he could to turn the situation around, but even his efforts proved fruitless.

I asked Jake Barnes what I could buy for the yard to make it better, and he told me to buy it a padlock, then to throw away the key. But I hate nothing more in life than giving up on a project, so we struggled on for a little longer. In the meantime, the Europeans had been losing money on Bayou Steel, so they sold out to a lead smelter who wanted to broker his own scrap. That was the last straw. With problems mounting and our business falling off, the horse wasn't worth the ride. We sold it.

CHAPTER THIRTEEN
THE NEXT GENERATION

With all the challenges facing Alter's scrap and barge business in 1980, I was overworked, overstressed, underexercised, and smoking eighty cigarettes a day. In fact, eighty a day wasn't enough for me. I'd wake up in the middle of the night to have a cigarette and I'd hold it between my fingers so that if I fell asleep, it would burn me awake before I started a fire.

When I suffered my heart attack, I was lucky it wasn't more severe. In fact, I thought it was just a bad case of indigestion. I even went climbing in the hills of Brazil and couldn't understand why I was so tired all the time. At my next annual physical, Dr. Goldman told me what had happened. Driving to Florida a year later, I was feeling so strange that Renee insisted I go to a hospital. The doctor told me I had angina and advised me to continue on to Florida, then relax. Relaxation didn't help. I could barely walk half a block without getting severe chest pains.

I took some tests at Mount Sinai Hospital, and the angiogram showed that two of my arteries were 98 percent blocked. I was scheduled for a heart bypass operation at once. The operation went well, and afterwards the doctors did a good job of scaring me into a new lifestyle. I quit smoking and determined to pass on much of my responsibility at Alter

Chuck Smith succeeded me as president of the scrap business.

*In the early 1980s, following heart trouble, I began spending
more time in Florida and less at Alter Company.*

Companies. Jake Barnes always said that important decisions at Alter were made by the *one man, one vote* system. I was the one man, joked Jake, and mine was the one vote. If that was ever true, it soon stopped being so. Step by step, I removed myself from management.

We separated our barge operation from our metal and brokerage businesses. That way, each could help the others when it was advantageous, but none would be seriously hurt when times were bad. Chuck Smith was appointed president of the scrap business and Gordon Jones president of Alter Barge. I started arriving at work later and leaving earlier. Renee and I bought a condo in Boca Raton and planned to spend

Gordon Jones succeeded me as president of Alter Barge Line.

two months each winter there. But the warm weather was seductive: the two months soon stretched into six, and the next thing we knew we'd taken up Florida residency.

In 1984, we appointed Dick Coonrod and Al Glazer as the first nonexecutive members to the Alter board. It was partly an inevitable consequence of Alter's growth and diversification, but my sons were coming up in the business, and so it was also an effort to preempt any repeat of the brotherly bust-ups that had caused so much grief to Morris and Harry, Frank and his two brothers, and Arant and me.

In 1984, Dick Coonrod (left) and Al Glazer (right) became Alter Company's first outside members of the board.

Fortunately, Jeff, Rob, and Rich have always gotten along better than I could have hoped, but Al Glazer and Dick Coonrod proved their worth in many other ways.

Al, an accountant and business advisor from Chicago, could scan a sheet of numbers and ask the right questions more quickly than anyone I've ever met. Dick, formerly vice president of Pillsbury's worldwide grain operations, understood trends, markets, and grain like no one else. They both knew a wide range of people and were experienced businessmen. Our board meetings became tremendous fun. On April 30 each year (the end of our fiscal year), we'd break out the bottle and all make predictions on what the following year promised for our markets and businesses. Then we'd read back our predictions from the year before, which was often a chastening experience.

I I

The time came for my sons to choose whether to go into the scrap business, the barge business, or something else. All three opted for scrap. With Gordon Jones looking forward to retiring and relandscaping the golf courses around Green Valley, Arizona, with his nine iron, that meant we badly needed a new leader for Alter Barge Line. I told Gordon that he could retire when he had found a replacement, as Eno had done. That got him busy, and in March 1982 we recruited John McKenzie from St. Louis. Sadly, by the time John joined us, the barge market had pretty much slipped into its thirteen-year coma. His main job was to keep us alive.

John found many cost-cutting opportunities. We ran as lean as possible. Crew numbers were cut back. Boats and barges coasted downstream to New Orleans whenever possible, to save fuel. At times, when rates were very low, we tied our barges up. At other times, we refused to run loads downstream unless there was a back haul available. The relationship between our scrap and barge interests was scrutinized. Scrap was physically damaging the barges, and we found we could hire other people's barges for lower rates. That freed up our own barges to be used more profitably elsewhere and also meant they lasted longer.

The recession was unrelenting. Unfortunately, barge companies enjoyed no strong industry association, but I argued strongly and publicly that the leading barge lines needed to work together to scrap excess barges or sell them overseas, and thereby trim oversupply and increase our chances of survival. But no one backed me up, everyone looked out for themselves, and we all suffered for it. Most independent barge lines either went bankrupt, consolidated, or sold big chunks of their fleet.

At last the recession bottomed out. It wasn't going to get better for awhile, but at least it wasn't worsening either. We knew we'd survived. More confident, we began to look around for opportunities to acquire assets. After all, we weren't the only ones who'd been hurt. There were plenty of bargains available, and over the following few years, we almost doubled our number of barges to 400. At the same time, we began looking to buy more river-related businesses, which we could bring in as part of Alter Transportation.

I I I

For many years, Wisconsin Barge Line owned and operated a river terminal in Rock Island called, logically enough, the Rock Island River Terminal. It was an integrated facility for transferring bulk commodities like road salt, pig iron, fertilizer, and animal feed supplements, from barge to rail, rail to truck, truck to barge, and back. It also provided some warehousing, storage, and handling. Though a solid enough business, Wisconsin Barge's management didn't sell it aggressively or maintain their property adequately. As a result, when the recession came, they started losing money. By 1980, they'd had enough.

We bought the business, rehired a few of their employees, and gave my son Rob the challenge of turning it around. He had a tough start. In his first week, the roof of one of the storage buildings collapsed in a rainstorm, and the animal feed inside, which had to be kept bone dry, was soaked. But he met that challenge, then set about renewing equipment, putting our buildings in shape, and building and strengthening our relationships with customers. Working well with his team, he built up a handling and bagging business, blowing animal feed pneumatically into fifty pound bags, stacking them on pallets, and shipping them out to the feed mixers. We also began bagging road salt and distributing it to local grocery and hardware stores, where it was sold for highways and driveways. We screened stoker coal to remove all the undersize pieces. Soon, the terminal was making a solid profit again and proving itself the business I'd hoped it would become.

Loading and unloading at Rock Island River Terminal in 1987.

Alter acquired Builder's Sand & Gravel in 1980 and sold the ready mix part in 1991.

IV

The Upper Mississippi around Davenport was served by just one switch boat company, Williams Marine. We'd helped Shorty Williams set up his business and remained very good customers of the company, even after Shorty passed away and his sons inherited. But when the barge industry went bad in the 1980s, and we asked Donn Williams and his brothers to cut their prices, they refused. So we decided they deserved some competition.

Builder's Sand & Gravel was an old Davenport concern that made its money dredging sand and gravel from the river and selling it, along with ready mix concrete and other building materials. The company had also accumulated some odd investments along the way, including a switch boat. Miss Delarue, its main stockholder and CEO, was a fine woman. She'd been the secretary of the business for awhile before inheriting it from its owner in the 1920s. She ran it for the next sixty years, well into her nineties. Her personality was so powerful that some people believe her spirit is still haunting the property, even though she died seventeen years ago.

I came into contact with her only once. She'd put an old locomotive crane on the railway track by the river, between her yard and ours. It had seen its last days years before, but she still kept it for some reason. One time, when the scrap market was very strong, I called her and offered her a very good price for the crane, intending to cut it up for scrap. "Young man," she replied, " that crane is there to keep you on your side of your property. I believe it's effective, and I intend to keep it."

Miss Delarue worked at her company right to the end, but after she died the whole company came up for sale. I only wanted to buy her dredge and switch boat, but to get it I ended up buying the whole company—including a grain and livestock farm. To my mother's horror, the farm had a large number of pigs on it (she was strictly kosher), as well as cows and sheep. When I suggested to my three sons that, should our manager fall ill, one of them would have to take over the farm, including milking the cows at five every morning, they decided that for the *strategic* good of the overall business, we should sell the farm. Ira Weindruch took over the management of the rest of the company, now renamed Builder's Sand & Cement, and built it substantially. He bought it from us in the fall of 1991.

As for the switch boat, we ran it as a separate venture. We had previously purchased a stretch of riverfront property south of Davenport, and we turned it into a barge parking lot called Blackhawk Fleet. We rented two more switch boats and later bought others from the Heritage Pullman Bank, naming them after our grandchildren. We now have *Michael*, *Marc*, *Lauren*, *Samantha*, *Joshua*, and *Nathan*, as well as the *Emily Kay*, named after Dick Coonrod's granddaughter. Renee is constantly reminding me to buy more switch boats, so as not to leave out our other three grandchildren, Jeremy, Alex, and Jesse.

With the boats, we switched our own barges around the Davenport and Muscatine areas. We did a pretty good job and won so much business away from Williams Marine that they eventually sold out, leaving us as the only local switch boat company. Unlike Williams, however, we took care never to get complacent with our monopoly, never to take advantage of our customers. People could rely on us to do what we had agreed to do. To this day, we act as though we're in a strongly competitive market, and that's why we're not.

The Marc, one of Alter's seven switch boats named for our grandchildren.

V

The Quad-City Container Terminal was another of our transport-related businesses, but we started this one from nothing more than an idea. The container revolution had changed the way freight was handled, and had, of course, created a tremendous need for containers. A brisk trade developed in shunting containers around the country and storing them until they were needed. Quad Cities businesses like John Deere, Alcoa, Honda, and others mostly used the container terminals in Chicago, until the Soo Line Railroad decided it would be viable to rail containers directly into the Quad Cities from the West and East Coasts. They made some detailed projections and forecasts, which looked promising and because the Iowa Department of Transportation was also encouraging the venture (it would save millions of gallons of gas every year), we agreed to set up, finance, and manage the Quad-City Container Terminal.

But the railroad never instituted freight rates that were competitive with Chicago, as they had promised, and so the business never picked up as predicted. Chicago was so close that many customers picked up their containers by truck as and when they needed them rather than using us. John McKenzie got back to the table with the Soo Line and the Iowa Department of Transportation to emphasize that their inaccurate estimates were costing us a great deal of money. We didn't let them go until we'd hammered out a guaranteed minimum business, which at least made the company viable.

Our grain brokerage initiative proved a more immediately profitable enterprise. We still had our "temporary" site on the Davenport seawall, where we'd started our

Moving containers at the Quad-City Container Terminal.

barge business. Over the years, we'd used it to store coal and salt, and as a grain facility to which corn and soybeans could be delivered by truck, weighed, stored, and loaded on barges. We subleased the property to Peavey Grain, but from 1980 onward the grain market suffered seven consecutive years of dropping sales. By 1986, Peavey had had enough. They left us with the choice of closing the business or running it ourselves.

There were good reasons to take it over. It was a solid business going through a bad time and would surely improve. Besides, owning it could help the flow of grain into our barges. There was also a terrible recession in the local farming community. I'd recently attended a conference of Midwest farmers in Kansas City, and in the hotel one night I overheard their wives complaining about the high prices of their dinner. They truly believed there were two sets of menus, one with reasonable prices for the locals and another to take advantage of gullible out-of-towners. That was when it really came home to me how tough the recession and the grain embargo had made life for our farmers. There was another reason, too. The grain companies had all been busy treading on my toes, getting themselves into the barge business. A bit of payback, it seemed to me, was only fair.

We named the company River/Gulf Grain, and hired Pat Grant from Continental Grain to run it. Pat Grant, and later Erol Melik, reported directly to me. The business essentially consisted of buying several million bushels of grain and soybeans a year from farmers in eastern Iowa and western Illinois, who trucked it in and dumped it directly into our bins. We then loaded our barges (or used other barge lines) and sailed the grain down to Louisiana, where it was sold to the major exporters.

Our timing was ideal. The year 1986 proved to be the low point for the grain industry, and from then on it started to recover. River/Gulf broke even in its first year and made a profit in its second. But then it tried to grow too big, too fast, expanding to the Iowa towns of Dubuque, Buffalo, Des Moines, and Clinton, using facilities in Rock Island, Illinois, and La Crosse, Wisconsin, and brokering through a dock in St. Louis. Before the market was strong enough to bear the overhead, we had bought or leased

Erol Melik became head of River/Gulf Grain in 1990.

*River/Gulf Grain can handle corn, beans,
and other bulk commodities.*

a great deal of property and hired many more employees. Our margins were too tight, and our profits slipped back into loss. It was time to slim down.

In 1990, we cut back the business to just twelve employees, and gave Erol Melik control. He soon made River/Gulf a success. He got back to basics, strengthening relationships with over one thousand local farmers, offering responsive account handling, and promising quick payments. We worked hard to improve our margins any way we could. We won back haul business for our trucks and arbitraged grain, hunting for premium prices. We forged strong links with the large grain processors and exporters. We leveraged Alter's reputation for honest dealing and financial strength to cut million-dollar deals over the phone. We also hedged extensively, buying and selling futures through the Chicago Grain Exchange. With 75 percent of Iowa and Illinois grain exported around the world, we needed to understand how good and bad harvests, crop conditions and qualities, and other factors affected the world grain markets. Our people learned well and soon made some sophisticated deals. One time, River/Gulf participated in a USDA-backed food-donation program, buying 2,200,000 bushels of corn, then supplying them (through a government-backed swap deal) to India.

V I

By the mid-1980s, our scrap business was also nearing a transition. My three sons, Jeff, Rob, and Rich, were all making good careers at Alter and showing the ability to lead. It is always a great privilege to see your children grow up into your business, but in a company like Alter, with nearly a thousand employees to consider, it is also a responsibility. My sons needed to know more, think harder, work longer, and be more courageous than anyone else. From their earliest years, Renee and I instilled the

Goldstein Family Honor (or GFH) system in our children, demanding absolute honesty from them. Violations of GFH were not tolerated. The system worked so well that it spread to other local families, and before long all the other children on our block used GFH!

As the boys reached their teens, I brought them to work in the yard during their holidays, where Willie Cooper and others showed them the ropes. I cut back their allowances, paid them half minimum wage, and taught them that money is more precious when it is earned. Later, when they joined Alter full-time, Chuck Smith became their mentor. Chuck, as always, did a fine job. He taught them the business, and at the same time he made certain they understood their responsibilities. After they'd graduated with honors from "Smith," I offered them the same freedom that Frank had once offered me—the chance to work in whichever area they thought they could contribute the most. They all started in scrap, and they've all done remarkably well.

Jeff started out at the St. Paul yard, where he learned the business from Alan Levey. After that, he came to Davenport to buy scrap for our new car shredder. He then worked in various areas of the company, including managing the Dubuque plant and a two year stint at Des Moines, before being assigned to deal with our nightmare yard in Louisiana. Now he's in charge of Valley Corporation, which manages our property interests around the Quad Cities. He is also now getting involved with River/Gulf Grain and our related transportation entities, including his recent appointment as president of Alter Barge Line.

Rob started in Davenport, where he soon earned promotion to superintendent. In 1980, he took charge of the Rock Island River Terminal, and later did similarly impressive work for our terminal network in Rock Island, LaCrosse, and St. Paul. He then took on a series of jobs, working in international brokerage and lobbying for riverboat gaming, before finally replacing Chuck Smith as head of Alter Trading. Rich started in Des Moines, then went to St. Paul and our Birmingham, Alabama, brokerage office, before working in New Orleans, Davenport, and then Dubuque. Now he's doing brokerage business in St. Louis.

As all three have taken on more and more responsibility, they've kept the Alter name as proud as ever. Time and time again, Jeff, Rob, and Rich have proved their intelligence, dedication, and leadership. I couldn't be prouder of them.

Of course, I'm just as proud of my daughter Kathy. She has a good mind, but she didn't have the same hankering to come into the business as the boys did. She spent a few weeks at the Davenport office during school holidays. One day, someone handed her some documents and asked her to "file them." Unfortunately, that was the exact same expression Renee used whenever she wanted something thrown out, so Kathy promptly tossed the papers in the trash.

Kathy married Arnie Millan, who worked in marketing. Arnie joined Alter and did a fine job running the Cedar Rapids yard. Next, he went into the nonferrous end and did pretty well there, too. Later, when we went into the gaming business, Arnie asked for a transfer to the *Diamond Lady* riverboat, where he worked on their marketing. I hired Dave Paltzik to work with him, and the two did a good job together. Eventually, however, Arnie resigned and he, Kathy, and their children moved to Seattle. They have since divorced.

Our daughter, Kathy Goldstein.

CHAPTER FOURTEEN
RIVERBOAT GAMING

At 7:15 on the morning of April 1, 1991, I smashed a bottle of champagne on the bow of the *Diamond Lady*, and so launched a new era of excursion and casino boats on the Mississippi River. ABC covered the event live, and the day-long celebrations were also broadcast nationally on CBS and CNN. Celebrities like Vanna White and Howard Keel joined me, my family, and thousands of Quad City citizens in the rebirth of riverboat gaming.

Launching riverboat gaming on the Mississippi River in 1991 was one of the proudest moments of my life.

·We acquired this J.I. Case Bettendorf property in 1988 and redeveloped it for riverboat gambling.

Standing on deck, that first morning, one of the journalists asked me whether I liked to gamble.

"Well," I laughed. "I'm gambling on this."

I never spoke a truer word. The next few years would be as exhilarating a roller coaster ride of success and disappointments as anything I had ever before experienced. And it came about like this:

After I'd handed over leadership of Alter Companies to Chuck Smith, Gordon Jones, John McKenzie, and my sons, I spent more and more time in Florida relaxing. But my golf game didn't improve and I didn't much enjoy walking the beach or sunbathing. I had enjoyed a financially successful life, yet now that I was retired and could afford to go to the finest restaurants and eat expensive meals, my doctor warned me not to eat steaks, or fat, or anything else that tasted good. Now that I could afford to buy myself a Cadillac and a Lexus, my doctor advised me not to drive, but to walk everywhere for the exercise. This was to be my reward for working hard all my life?

I didn't think so. I became restless. I had spent a lifetime working, and retirement wasn't easy for me. On the other hand, I'd have been a fool to return to Alter. Business had prospered without me, and my return would only harm it.

The Quad Cities had meanwhile fallen into a deep recession. Companies were folding all over town, and one in five residents were unemployed. Some grimly humorous bumper stickers started appearing, proclaiming things like "Last one out of town, please turn off the lights." As part of the recession, Tenneco closed its J.I. Case Bettendorf plant and put up for sale the 100-acre site, a mile-long strip along the Bettendorf riverfront adjacent to the I-74 bridge.

We had no plans for the property, but it was prime real estate, and we were wary of letting another switch boat line acquire it. Besides, we'd talked over the years of creating a major waterways terminal around the Quad Cities, where towboats and barges would come for repairs, as well as loading and unloading, with rail, truck, and storage facilities. Maybe this was our chance. Or perhaps we could turn it into a business park of small manufacturing units, warehouses, and offices (although at the time, John Deere, Caterpillar, and everyone else were cutting back staff, and they needed more office space like a hole in the head).

All in all, the site was worth owning, so we set up Green Bridge Company in 1988 and bought the property for $2 million, with Tenneco keeping responsibility for any future environmental liabilities. In 1990, we moved Alter's head offices from the Davenport yard into our new Bettendorf site.

Mayor Ann Hutchinson suggested we build shops and boutiques so that the public could enjoy the riverfront. I told her we'd have to find a way to attract more people than just the Quad City population. We soon found a way.

II

About the time we were finalizing the deal, Art Ollie, a legislator from Clinton, was considering ways to get some investment back into his community, tapping the heritage of the Mississippi River and Mark Twain. He had come up with the idea of riverboat gambling excursion trips. Bob Arnould, Speaker of the Democrat-led Iowa House, and Tom Fey, one of his Democrat colleagues, picked up on the idea, took it to the Iowa state legislature, and fought to make Iowa the only state between Nevada and New Jersey that allowed gambling. Trouble was, there wasn't much chance of their bill passing. All they had was an idea, and the legislature thought it was no good. They couldn't see the benefits, and had totally unfounded fears of an unholy influx of immorality, gambling addiction, crime, prostitution, and other horrors. Arnould and Fey needed evidence that gaming would boost the economy without damaging the society. They needed someone to show Iowa what an opportunity the riverboats could be.

When I heard about the scheme in the fall of 1988, it caught my imagination. After all, we were Iowa's only barge line, and we knew the Upper Mississippi like nobody else. Our safety record was the best of any barge line in America, according to our insurance companies. We also now owned the J.I. Case property, which was ideally located for such a venture. Riverboat excursions with gambling would bring in the numbers of people I had told the mayor we would need in order to develop the riverfront.

Most people thought I had retired from business, and I thought I had half retired, but suddenly the challenge of this new industry was too great to ignore. I had to take it on, despite my heart problems and my age, which forced me to do more and more by working through other people, rather than doing it myself, as I'd always done before. It was like the mountain that towers ahead of the mountain climber. Sixty years earlier, George Mallory had been asked repeatedly why he wanted to climb Mount Everest: "Because it is there," he answered. I know how he felt. Riverboat gaming was a challenge I just couldn't resist. I was looking for fun, and I found it.

I hired a gaming consultant to study the legislation. The bad news was that the proposed legislation would put gaming into a straitjacket, limiting bets to $5 and losses to $200 per cruise. Worse, they wanted to coop all the gamblers, tables, and slots in less than a third of the floor space. But there was good news, too. So long as no other states permitted gaming, we could expect to attract a bonanza of *eight million* new tourists to the Quad Cities each year. Those visitors would need rooms, food, and entertainment. I wanted Alter to give it to them, so we put together a serious business plan, envisioning a casino dock with a Mississippi theme park, new hotels, shops, restaurants, and a recreational vehicle park. We even talked to the railroads about running riverview trains between Davenport and Bettendorf, then Muscatine and Clinton.

Campaign pins for the launch of riverboat gaming in 1990.

Quad-City Times

149,500 readers and growing!   Copyright, 1989

VICTORS REJOICE — Three of the foremost proponents of riverboat gambling — Davenport Mayor Thom Hart and Iowa Reps. Tom Fey and Bob Arnould — savor the victory. (QUAD-CITY TIMES photo by Greg Boll)
Other reaction: Page 6

DEAL US IN!

River gambling wins by big margins

What's in the cards

By Rod Thomson
Linda Barr
and Clark Kauffman
QUAD-CITY TIMES

A CLEAN SWEEP

The Quad-City Times *celebrated the arrival of riverboat gaming in 1989.*

While Curt Beason, our counsel, led our lobbying effort with my son Rob, I sold our vision on local television and in a series of newspaper interviews. Whenever I could, I tried to add a touch of humor to our message. When I gave an impassioned speech to a Rotary Club in Scott County, I detailed all the reasons why the vote mattered so greatly to the local community and why all our supporters should therefore spare no effort to make sure they and their friends and families found time to vote in the crucial referendum. "But if you're against gaming," I added, "please don't vote at all." That got a good laugh.

The campaign turned me into a popular local celebrity, giving speeches and signing T-shirts, but still I had no idea how public and visible our family involvement would soon become. No one cared about our scrap or barges, but they loved gambling, theme parks, and excursion boats. And they loved the idea of new jobs.

The day of the vote neared, with the majority of legislators still against us. Curt and Rob redoubled our lobbying, winning crucial support vote by painful vote. When the count was returned from the Iowa House, our bill had squeaked through by a single vote. We held our breaths for the returns from the Senate. It had passed again, also by one vote. Our exhausting lobbying effort had paid off. Riverboat gaming was now legal in Iowa, and I'd earned myself celebrity status as a local hero and the title of "Father of Riverboat Gaming."

III

Even as Iowa was considering the riverboat gaming bill, we were preparing ourselves in case it passed. In mid-1989, I received a phone call from John Connelly, a Pittsburgh promoter and operator of excursion boats who had an old excursion boat called the *President*. He had heard about the riverboat gaming legislation, and he suggested a joint venture. It sounded like a great opportunity, so I went to see his Pittsburgh operation, which impressed me, and then we flew on his private jet to St. Louis to see the *President*.

The moment I saw it, my heart sank. The boat was sixty-seven years old, and it looked every creaking day of it. Its paddle wheels had been replaced with diesel engine outboards, housed in two engine rooms, one on each side. When I asked to see the engine rooms, Connelly said he was a marketer, not an engineer, so he asked Israel "Izzy" Gorman, a crew member, to show me. Izzy knew the boat like nobody else. He had lived aboard it since he was eleven. But what he showed me was even more depressing. Much of the steel plate was so rusted and pitted that the only reason to purchase it would have been for scrap. I told Connelly it made more sense to commission new boats. I offered him a partnership and told him I'd send him the numbers as soon as we could develop them.

It was time to build a team and some boats. Doug Kratz, who was then CFO of Alter Company, became the first president of the new enterprise. He was a very dynamic man, who walked fast, talked fast, and accomplished a tremendous amount for us before he left to run the Rock Island Bank. We were all very sorry to see him go. I also recruited Tim Hinkley to run our food and beverage operations, and Robert Gensamer to manage gaming. My then son-in-law, Arnie Millan, headed up marketing. With people in place, we commissioned two boats, the

Doug Kratz, former CFO of Alter Company, became first president of Steamboat.

Building the paddle wheel of one of our new boats in Jacksonville, Florida, in 1990.

Diamond Lady and the *Emerald Lady*, to be designed by John Gilbert and built by Atlantic Marine in Jacksonville, Florida. We wanted them to be stunning and to replicate the authentic 1800s feel, yet still surpass U.S. Coast Guard standards. That was neither easy nor cheap, but we spared no expense in their design.

Each was a 1,200-ton, 201-foot-long sternwheeler, powered with three 670-horsepower engines. Each could accommodate one thousand passengers on its three decks and was capable of cruising at fourteen knots. They were fast, safe, and easy to maneuver through locks and dams. They were painted white with red, blue, and black trim. In painstaking detail, they faithfully reproduced the elegance, style, and look of the old riverboats, down to the graceful Victorian decor, paddle wheels, gangways, and even the camber of the decks. They were luxuriously furnished and beautifully appointed with Philippine mahogany, chrome bar stations, marble counter tops, carved glass panels, and crystal chandeliers. Each had a calliope for music and a dais for a band. Their dining rooms were a proud focal point: elegant, plush, ornate, and offering a sumptuous menu. Everything was set. All we were waiting for were licenses.

Around this time, Rock Island and Moline, Illinois, announced they didn't want to be left out of the Quad Cities' gaming future and wanted riverboat gaming for themselves. It was a terrible shock, because it would open up the whole state of Illinois to casinos, and a great number of our anticipated customer base would be coming from Chicago or St. Louis. If there were casinos in Peoria and Joliet, for example,

Chicago customers would not bother to travel all the way to the Quad Cities. Likewise, if there were a casino in Alton or East St. Louis, people from Missouri would simply cross the river, not come up it. The bombshell news blew so big a hole in our estimates, I could have sailed the *Diamond Lady* through it. Forget eight million tourists! We'd be lucky to get eight hundred thousand, and most of those would be locals, driving in for the evening, who wouldn't need hotel rooms. My hopes of constructing a theme park, hotels, railroad shuttle, and an RV park were crumbling.

We tried to fight the Illinois legislation. The independent Quad Cities *Vision for the Future* published figures backing up our statements and predictions, but those were ridiculed by the local press. It was no consolation that those estimates were later proved correct, and that the whole of the Quad Cities suffered for it. Rob went to an open meeting in Illinois and warned people in Moline and Rock Island that by pushing for casinos in Illinois, they were endangering the goose that would lay golden eggs for the whole Quad City area. But Rock Island and Moline people simply accused us of being greedy, trying to hog the market.

Illinois State Senator Denny Jacobs was one of the most vociferous supporters of the bill, claiming that Illinois needed to "beat" Iowa on the bill. That was so negative, I went head-to-head with him on the subject. Although I showed him how the Illinois legislation would destroy most of the prospects for the Quad Cities and endanger the new theme park, hotels, and other construction, he said that he represented the whole state of Illinois, not just Moline and Rock Island. His shortsightedness angered me. He wanted it for the Illinois side of the Quad Cities, and as a result, neither side was going to get much.

That's how it worked out, too. Illinois did pass the legislation, and as a result the Quad Cities never got the bonanza for which I had worked so hard. Even today, whenever I'm in the Quad Cities, I can see that the riverboat casinos have been very good for the area. They've increased employment, tourism, morale, and the whole economy, but I know the increase could have been ten times greater. I still imagine how it might have been had Denny Jacobs and his Illinois friends not pushed for gaming. Billions of dollars would have been invested in the region. There would have been hundreds of new restaurants and businesses, thousands of new hotel rooms, and tens of thousands of new jobs—on both sides of the Mississippi. The influx of tourists would have demanded improved air, road, and rail facilities and massive investment in entertainment, from a theme park to golf courses, horse tracks, and other facilities. The Quad Cities would have been a boom town, one of the great success stories of the decade, and maybe even of the new millennium. Instead, thanks to the Illinois legislation, other cities are reaping the rewards. People from the region just don't realize what they've missed.

For our own part, the proposed legislation had one more downside. Fearing that Illinois casinos would impact the number of our customers, I decided to cut the size of the *Diamond Lady* and the *Emerald Lady*. It made good sense to me at the time, but it soon proved to be a bad mistake.

I V

The Iowa Racing & Gaming Commission was due to award licenses on March 8, 1990. As part of their process, they conducted extensive background checks on me, my family, and my companies. They found us fit to operate casinos, as Illinois, Mississippi, and Louisiana would later also do. Incidentally, the popular belief that casinos are still run by hoodlums and Mafiosi is completely wrong—the investigation is so thorough, your past had better be cleaner than clean if you want to qualify for a license.

While we concentrated on our bids for the Quad Cities, other small southeast Iowa towns like Muscatine, Keokuk, and Clinton were all after us to put them on our cruise schedule. They promised to do everything they could to make our boats welcome, but we warned them not to undertake any projects on our behalf. We also began successful negotiations for a license from Sioux City, and consequently placed a third boat, the *Golden Lady*, on order. But we made it clear that we were only interested in investing in Sioux City if we were the only casino in western Iowa. Then we discovered that representatives of an Indian tribe from Nebraska, which owned land in Iowa, were negotiating a casino of their own on their land just south of Sioux City. No one who knew had seen fit to inform us. We immediately returned our license, which did little for our popularity, but our place was taken by a local group who lost money from the moment the Indian casino opened. That still left us with a problem, however. The *Golden Lady* was already being built, and we had nowhere to put it.

Meanwhile, lobbying for licenses in Davenport was becoming intense. Delta Queen offered to refurbish a boat they owned, but wouldn't commit any money to land-based developments. Frank Freid and Harry Belafonte made a big song and dance about all the wonderful things they'd do, then promptly vanished. My one-time prospective partner, John Connelly, also came to Davenport, but not on my behalf. I still thought he wanted to work with me, but behind my back, he met with local aldermen and started campaigning. He'd got the *President* recertified by the Coast Guard, which I'll bet cost him a fortune. Now he made a verbal promise to invest $100 million in a new hotel and insinuated that, while he was a professional who knew how to deal with the public, Bernie Goldstein was a junk dealer who knew nothing about gaming or entertainment.

Finally, Connelly's campaign came out into the open, and things really heated up. Connelly addressed the Davenport Rotary Club and remarked that between a Connelly and a Goldstein, Jesus was surely on his side. He also won over most of the newspapers, including the *Quad-City Times*. Whenever they published a picture of Connelly, he was smiling like a favorite uncle, but whenever they published anything about me, my picture was frowning and scowling. Connelly was a master of politicking, and he outmaneuvered me in my own town. His promise of a $100-million hotel investment (as opposed to our firm commitment of $50 million) swayed the Davenport City Council. The *President* was recommended by Davenport, although not unanimously, and was duly awarded the gaming license for the city of Davenport. Connelly never did build his new hotel, of course, but bought the old Blackhawk Hotel instead.

Now we had a choice—half a loaf or none at all. Should we go for Bettendorf or give up? We went ahead, and Steamboat Development Company was awarded two licenses. The *Diamond Lady* would cruise between Bettendorf, Muscatine, and Clinton, while the *Emerald Lady* offered service between Burlington, Fort Madison, and Keokuk. Finally, Robert Kehl, who operated excursion boats along the Upper Mississippi, was awarded the license to operate the *Casino Belle* in Dubuque's Ice Harbor.

The boats were to open in a little over a year, on April 1, 1991. April Fools' Day.

Just three weeks after the licenses were handed out, Renee and I were at our Bettendorf home getting ready to go to bed. All of a sudden, Renee cried out in agony, screaming terribly. I called 911 and asked for an ambulance. A few minutes later, a fire engine arrived. Thinking the emergency people had made a mistake, I told them that there was no fire. "God damn it," I said "We need an ambulance, now." But the mistake was mine. The fire crew rushed past me and gave Renee life-saving oxygen.

The ambulance arrived moments later and rushed Renee to hospital. I was told she had suffered a brain aneurysm, which meant that an artery had burst in her brain. It was often fatal, I learned, or if not, it usually meant strokes and possibly paralysis. On medical advice, we got a helicopter to fly Renee to the State University Hospital in Iowa City, where Doctor Van Gilder, one of the top specialists in the country, performed the brain surgery. Even with his expertise, Renee was in intensive care for a full week before we knew she would pull through. Still, we did not know how completely she would recover.

We brought Renee home after two months and had nurses and therapists in the house around the clock as she began an intensive rehabilitation program. She needed to learn how to do all those things controlled by the part of her brain that had been affected, including how to walk again. (That part of the brain also controlled arithmetic, but I tell everybody that was no problem since she was never very good at it anyway—she laughs every time I tell the story.) The speech therapy was so tough, she kept throwing the therapists out of the house; but thankfully we found one who kept at it, and the hard work paid wonderful dividends. To this day, and despite her complete recovery, Renee can't remember a thing about those four horrible months.

V

By March 1991, the ice on the Upper Mississippi had begun to thaw and break up, and as we prepared the *Diamond Lady* to sail from Jacksonville to Bettendorf, the excitement in the Quad Cities was palpable. At last the Quad Cities had something to laugh and smile about, and it was a pleasure to be part of it.

A CHANCE TO SAIL   **6B** MONDAY, OCTOBER 29, 1990
                                              THE MIAMI HERALD

The Diamond Lady *was launched at Atlantic Marine in Jacksonville in October 1990.*

The race up the Mississippi caught the public imagination. Naturally, all three ventures wanted their boats to arrive in Iowa first and be the first to open. John Connelly's *President* had a head start. After all, it was only sailing from New Orleans, while the *Diamond Lady* had to sail all the way from Jacksonville, Florida. But the *Diamond Lady* was far faster than the *President*. Its modern engines quickly made up the time. Local papers started featuring the race. Soon, the *Diamond Lady* caught up with the *President*, then overtook it. The race turned into a celebration. In town after town, day and night, the banks of the Mississippi River were jammed with people cheering on our *Diamond Lady*, its big red paddle wheel spinning, its flags flying, and music pouring from its calliope.

On March 17, the *Diamond Lady* reached Bettendorf. Alan "Doc" Hathaway, a good friend, led his Dixieland band as they played in our dining area, the musicians decked out in red-and-white striped shirts and white pants. Our jetty on the

Alan "Doc" Hathaway and his Dixieland band.

J.I. Case property wasn't ready, so Bettendorf rented us the riverfront property previously rented to Robert Kehl. As a competitor, he wasn't too happy about that, so he launched a lawsuit against Steamboat and the city of Bettendorf, which failed.

We built parking space nearby and provided buses to shuttle guests to the covered ramp of the boat and back. A last minute Coast Guard check found the *Diamond Lady* fit to sail. As the countdown continued, local interest became frantic. Every edition of every local newspaper seemed to carry some story or other. Our reservations system was so overwhelmed by the number of calls and booking requests that the entire phone system to Bettendorf clogged up!

April 1 finally arrived, opening day for the casinos. We wanted to beat John Connelly and Bob Kehl to the start. Kehl didn't prove much of a challenge. His *Casino Belle* wasn't even expected to reach Dubuque until the afternoon. Connelly's *President* was a different matter altogether. Its first cruise was scheduled for 9:00 a.m., which Connelly thought would make it first; but we had other plans.

At 6:30 a.m., Renee and I arrived at Leach Park in a horse-drawn carriage. There was already a crush of journalists and a crowd of hundreds waiting. It was a beautiful spring morning, with clear ice-blue skies. As I arrived, it was still cold and crisp, but there was enough electricity in the air to keep everybody warm. "This isn't Las Vegas or Atlantic City," I told the crowd. "This is something uniquely born right here in the Mississippi River Valley. I think you'll find it's even better."

At 7:15 a.m., we staged a simulated launch for ABC television's "Good Morning America" program. I smashed a bottle of champagne on the bow and drenched my socks. Then we began to board for real, and at 7:45 a.m., we set off on our maiden cruise. The *Diamond Lady's* captain, Charles K. Murphy, a 17-year Alter veteran, sailed us downriver to the Oneida Street Landing in Davenport, while the Reverend Joe Roost played "Waitin' for the Robert E. Lee" on the calliope. The Quad Cities' own Howard Keel, the singer-actor, and 1991's Miss Iowa were among five hundred people on board for the first cruise. Howard set the gaming going when he threw seven with a pair of golden dice on the craps table. Jeff and Helen Weindruch were the first to place bets, winning $7 on their first roll. Soon, the tables and the slot machines were crowded with enthusiastic gamblers. I stood and watched, drinking it all in.

People kept coming up to me, asking me what they should do. I know how to bet a few dollars on craps or blackjack or a horse, but I'm no expert on gambling. Yet because I'm in the business, people always ask me how they can win. Over the years, I've come up with an answer that makes people laugh every time: "Be lucky," I say. That night, I felt lucky. A dream had come true for me. My *Diamond Lady* had just become the first riverboat casino in modern American history.

The celebrations lasted all day and night. Our guests raved about the experience, and about the boat. Each time we returned to the riverside, hundreds and hundreds of eager people greeted us with cheers and applause. As long lines of people formed on the riverside, Clesen Havill Smith, a convincing Mark Twain look-alike, and a southern

Vanna White and I at the Diamond Lady's wheel of fortune in April 1991.

belle in a hoop skirt welcomed them on board. Celebrities and leading citizens from the Quad Cities flocked to the gala evening. The media people asked Vanna White, the beautiful co-host of "Wheel of Fortune," to spin our own wheel of fortune. I gave her a $5 chip to bet, and she put it on 20-1 and promptly won herself $100. Very kindly, she then returned my $5 to me. It was a good omen, though, and a great evening. The *Diamond Lady* was the toast of the town.

It was one of the proudest moments of my life.

VI

On May 9, 1991, our second boat, the *Emerald Lady*, sailed into Burlington, Iowa, to the cheers of another huge crowd. The following day, fireworks celebrated her passage to Fort Madison and Keokuk, and William Warfield of Champaign, Illinois, sang an a cappella rendition of "Old Man River," his hit song from the 1951 Broadway musical *Showboat*, that made the hairs on my arms stand on end.

Fort Madison served up a huge 760-pound cake shaped like a riverboat. It also served up a less welcome surprise. It was the first time I'd visited the town since the

The Emerald Lady *on the Mississippi River.*

licenses had been awarded, and the riverfront had been extensively developed. The improvements weren't necessary for our operations, and I hoped the council hadn't made them on our behalf. The last thing we needed was for towns to get overexcited about the boats and put themselves into unnecessary debt. To my relief, I was reassured that the improvements were wanted anyway. Even so, they'd soon return to haunt us.

Our boats did very well for a while, and our excursions were much enjoyed. We sailed a beautiful stretch of the Upper Mississippi, with Steamboat staffers providing historical narratives. Our investment had been huge, but it seemed it might pay off. Then the novelty began to wear thin, and the number of our customers began to fall, particularly during the week and in the mornings. We got our first financial returns, and they made grim reading. We realized we'd made some mistakes and misjudgments. We had hired too many crew, and our whole reservations system was unnecessary. We should have operated on a first-come, first-served basis.

We'd also tried too hard to recapture the true Mississippi riverboat experience. The authentic camber in our decks made it difficult to set slot machines flat. We'd also saved money in the wrong places, leasing second-hand slot machines and gaming tables, when we should have invested in new. There was worse. Fearing future Illinois competition, I had reduced the size of our boats. It saved us very little construction money, but it turned the boats into lousy casinos. They were too small to meet weekend demand, and Friday night and Saturday night business proved critical to success. John Connelly's *President* was a lousy cruise boat but a great casino. It had space for gaming, and on Saturday nights, gaming space was all that mattered.

Our boats faced other more general problems. The $5 bet and $200 excursion limits were dampening excitement. The excursions were not the draw we'd hoped. In fact, to many customers they were a curse. The *Diamond Lady* sailed from Bettendorf to Muscatine, then back to Bettendorf. The trips lasted four hours or more. We had eliminated Clinton from the *Diamond Lady's* schedule before we even started, because Robert Kehl had also gotten a license there over our objections. The *Emerald Lady* ran between Burlington, Fort Madison, and Keokuk. Guests were taken miles away from their cars, then offered a bus ride or a second cruise. The buses were not popular, and that could mean more than eight hours on board, too much for most people.

We therefore changed our cruising schedule, allocating the boats to different towns on different days of the week. Instead of operating cruises between the towns, we ran local excursions of an hour and a half, returning to the dock for disembarkation. Despite the euphoria of our opening nights and our efforts at reorganization, business didn't improve. Our gaming company began losing so much money that we had to take cash out of other family companies to cover its losses, and our management meetings grew increasingly gloomy.

Steamboat was sinking fast.

CHAPTER FIFTEEN
OUT OF STATE

In 1991, as we had feared, the state of Illinois passed gaming legislation. What we hadn't expected was that the legislation allowed gambling *without limits*. This was something that apparently shocked even the Illinois legislature. Denny Jacobs blamed it on a secretarial mistake! Sure! We knew at once that we couldn't compete with limit-free Illinois casinos, not unless we could go limit-free ourselves. We asked our legislators for help, but they told us they couldn't do anything, "not in an election year." Besides, they said, the *Quad-City Times* was for keeping the limits, and so was the *President*. Or maybe they just wanted to squeeze their competition out of business.

Sadly, our predictions about the impact of Illinois casinos soon proved correct. Instead of eight million tourists, the Quad Cities would attract just eight hundred thousand, and those were mostly locals who didn't need hotel rooms or RV parks.

Well, if you can't beat 'em, join 'em. Dale Burklund, a citizen of Peoria, Illinois, came to me with the idea of putting a boat into Peoria. It made sense. After all, we had already ordered the *Golden Lady*, originally intended for Sioux City, and we had to do something with it. Dale became chairman of the board of the new venture, and he and some other local investors took 75 percent of the equity. The remaining equity was split among my sons and daughter, Chuck Smith, Jake Barnes, my nephew Jim Goldstone, and Bob Ellis, my niece's husband. (Bob is a doctor, and not to be

Chuck Smith and Jake Barnes on the deck of the Diamond Lady.

confused with another Bob Ellis, our in-house counsel.) Together, we applied for and won the license for East Peoria, Illinois. It was the first license awarded in the state, but this time we were beaten to the opening by a converted excursion boat in Alton, Illinois. We renamed the Golden Lady the *Par-A-Dice*, after an old, illegal, Peoria gaming joint. We built it bigger than the *Ladies*, and it proved a far better casino. We also ran the operation differently, serving only one port and setting up a company to manage everything from training the dealers to running the restaurants, for a percentage of the gross. We looked to expand the concept into Galena, and also had ambitions for Joliet and East St. Louis.

But expansion in Illinois wasn't simple. The state had a rule limiting casino ownership, stating that no person with 10 percent or more of any one casino could be involved in any other. Because we wanted multiple licenses in Illinois, we asked Mort Friedman, executive director for the Illinois Gaming Commission, to clarify that rule when we established ourselves in Peoria. Based on conversations with him, I didn't invest at all in Peoria, and I restricted my sons' and daughter's interest to less than 10 percent. But I encouraged other colleagues from Alter Company to invest.

Excited about our prospects in Joliet and East St. Louis, we invested significant time and money, designing a harbor for Joliet, planning boats, lobbying, and making

The Par-A-Dice, in East Peoria, Illinois. The boat, named after an old illegal gaming joint, was owned with a group primarily from Illinois.

preparations. Again, based on conversations with Mort, Jeff, Rob, Rich, and Kathy and her husband Arnie, each took 10 percent in the bidding company for Joliet, and we invited hotelier John Q. Hammons to take the remaining shares.

When I arrived in Chicago two days before the licenses were awarded, Mort told me he'd reread the gaming law and had changed his mind 180 degrees as to what it meant. Because my four children, two nephews, and two employees each held stakes in Peoria, and because Renee and I owned the managing company, he now maintained that we were cumulatively over the 10 percent limit. According to Mort, that made us ineligible for Joliet or East St. Louis. Joliet would prove to be tremendously profitable because of its location on the edge of Chicago. It was so good that its returns even shocked Harrah's, one of the world's leading casino companies. East St. Louis, which I had planned to bid for with Renee, also proved an outstanding license. We lost them both, because we followed advice from the executive director of the state's gaming commission. We also wasted a great deal of time and money planning our bids.

As if he hadn't done us enough damage, Mort then decided to come after our Peoria operation. After six months of intensive investigation, he discovered the shocking fact that Peoria had bought and rented training equipment from our Bettendorf training school—a transaction that had been reported to, and cleared by, the Illinois states attorney. Even so, Mort pursued it like a mutt chasing after an ankle, claiming we'd violated the law, threatening us with fines and even with revoking our license.

Our lawyers assured us we would win in court, but warned that the case might not be resolved for two or three years—and that any unsettled litigation would effectively prevent us from successfully pursuing licenses in other states. We had to settle quickly, so we authorized our lawyers to make a compromise under which the Peoria management company paid $250,000, and Jeff, Rob, Rich, Kathy, my wife, and I each paid $5,000. Most important, the agreement acknowledged our position—that my family did nothing wrong, and that we did not even know of the questioned transaction. We did not and would not admit to any wrongdoing, as we'd done none.

By now it was clear that we had no future in Illinois so long as Mort sat in the gaming commissioner's chair, so we pulled back from making any more bids, sold the management company, and eventually pulled out of Illinois altogether. In 1996, *Par-A-Dice* was sold to Boyd Gaming for $175 million, a tremendous return for our partners of their initial investment of around $12 million. Over the years I've been in business, I have gone into several partnerships. I pride myself that every one of my partners always made money. This includes the Davis family, in Midland Iron & Metal, my friend Ira Weindruch, my friends Norm and Marty Rich in a barge chartering partnership, and the original Anubis investors who merged into the beginning of Casino America. Our partners in *Par-A-Dice* clearly did especially well, getting back more than ten times their original investment.

Incidentally, my desire to ensure that my partners always made money from our ventures together was one reason why we didn't take any partners when we invested in the *Diamond Lady* and *Emerald Lady*. At that time, the deal was too risky to involve others. We didn't know enough about the business. There were chances to be taken, and that meant I just couldn't risk other people's money.

I I

With Illinois casinos pulling in the gamblers and profits, our riverboats in Iowa lost even more money. Ed Ernst, who was part of our team as a partner in McGladrey & Pullen (Alter's accountants), came in to try and turn the situation around, but it only became increasingly clear that our efforts in Iowa had failed. There was nothing left to try. In the end, while the *Ladies* contributed more than $7 million to the state of Iowa, local communities, and charities, they lost over $10 million in operations.

We had a stark choice. One option was to put the Steamboat Companies into bankruptcy, but I wouldn't allow that. Alter companies never ran from their obligations. Another option was to sell our boats to others. We looked hard at that option but couldn't find a buyer. Our third option was to move our boats to a more profitable site and work to pay off our debts.

Allan Solomon, one of the founding directors of Casino America.

By now, Mississippi and Louisiana had also legalized gaming. Legislation was also pending in Missouri. Mississippi seemed an attractive prospect, not least because the state didn't require that casinos must cruise. An influential Mississippi restaurateur had wanted on-board gaming, but his barge restaurant had no engine. No problem. He'd just lobbied until he won the right legislation.

I notified the Iowa Racing & Gaming Commission that we were considering a move. It didn't come as much of a surprise to them, because they'd seen our accounts and knew that we were struggling for cash. We didn't even have enough money to finance a move, so Allan Solomon and Ed Ernst went to Sheldon Fleck, a Minneapolis entrepreneur, and, with $3 million in cash, arranged to merge some of our riverboat management operations into a small, nonoperating public company that Sheldon had available. We called it Casino America.

III

Now that we were considering bidding for casino licenses in other states, we started scouting for potential sites. I'd been looking for riverfront property for scrap yards for many years, so I knew the importance of a navigable river and good road access. While others looked in downtown areas, I kept to the suburbs, looking at the junctions of rivers and interstate highways. The policy had always worked well for car bodies and, over the next few years, it proved that it could work for human bodies, too.

We took an option on a riverfront property in Natchez, Mississippi, signed a letter of intent with Mr. Biglane, the landlord, and then were awarded the first license in Mississippi. The property was far from ideal, however. Natchez was on a high bluff overlooking the Mississippi River, and there was no easy route down to its banks. The currents ran dangerously fast, and the river could rise sixty feet when in flood. Creating good access to a safely moored boat was going to be a real engineering challenge. But we never found out if we were up to it, because Mr. Biglane unilaterally tore up our letter of intent. We sought legal advice and were advised that we had no chance of winning a decision against a Mississippi native in a Mississippi court.

I visited Natchez anyway, to see if there might be another suitable property, but without success. Instead, the day I went to Natchez to tell the mayor that we were pulling out was the day after Harrison County, Mississippi, approved riverboat gaming. Our lawyer, Wilson Golden, was with me. He knew about the approval, and also knew the mayor of Biloxi, Harrison County's county seat. After we left Natchez City Hall, therefore, I asked Wilson to drive the two hundred miles to Biloxi.

Biloxi had been a leading resort town of the "Redneck Riviera" for many decades—in fact, Renee and I had visited it on our honeymoon—but it was suffering now. Hurricane Camille had had a devastating impact in 1969, while the relatively new I-10 took motorists right past it, to Florida and elsewhere. Biloxi's hotels and golf courses were dilapidated, and there were seedy shops everywhere. Business was so bad that even the Burger King closed down for the winter. Even so, the moment I drove into the town and saw waves breaking on the long, white-sand beaches, I knew it was a far better prospect than Natchez. And the locals, desperate for good investment and decent jobs, welcomed us like saviors.

We found a fine piece of city-owned property at the easternmost point of Biloxi, called Point Cadet. On May 27, 1992, within days of arriving in Biloxi, we'd struck a deal. But things were happening much faster than expected. When we appeared in Mississippi before the three-person taxing and gaming commission, we had no idea we would be granted the license. Our site was next door to Mississippi Union Aquarium and they were not on our side. But an impassioned plea by Mayor Halet describing the area's high unemployment, lack of opportunities, and other local economic hardships led to a 2 to 1 vote giving us the license.

Then the chairman of the Gaming Commission asked Ed Ernst and me when we would be ready to open. We told him August 1, but begged for a few days to explain our situation to the Quad Cities. He refused. If we didn't make the announcement that very same day, he said, he'd do so himself. With no choice, Ed Ernst and I called a press conference in Jackson, Mississippi, for that same afternoon and announced by phone to the Quad Cities media that we'd be sailing the *Diamond Lady* and *Emerald Lady* to Biloxi on July 6, and that a new public company, Casino America, would be taking over the boats.

The media response was horrible. Where once I was the local hero, I was now a con artist. I can understand why the abruptness of the announcement upset many people in the Quad Cities and caused anxiety to employees on our boats, but I cannot understand why the media were so one-sided. The Associated Press published an article calling me the "Music Man," after the celebrated musical in which a con man fools the citizens of an Iowa town out of their savings. But I was the one who lost $10 million, while local nonprofits, the state of Iowa, and surrounding cities actually made $7 million. Go figure! Other newspapers painted me as some kind of villain, claiming I wanted to make more money elsewhere, as if I had been making money in Iowa. I wish!

I wouldn't have minded so much, but few of the journalists who criticized me made any effort to find out my side of the story; and one or two went way too far, printing lies or twisting the few facts they did have like a wet towel, squeezing every possible drop of malice out of them. Certainly, those who knew the situation understood that we'd done everything we could to make our Iowa casinos work, but the plain truth is that sometimes things fail, despite best intentions and hardest efforts. That's how we failed at Steamboat.

The bad press coverage continued even to 1997, when the *Des Moines Register* published a horrible article by (the now-retired) James Flansburg. Casino America was hoping that Dallas County, Iowa, would approve riverboat casinos so that we could construct a casino hotel project at Clearwater Lake in their county. Just before the vote,

Flansburg accused me of all kinds of things, without merit or cause, and without bothering to check. I could have brought a successful libel suit against the paper, but that would have been costly, aggravating, and time-consuming. Instead, Dennis Ryerson, chief editor, was courteous enough to publish an article I wrote, finally telling my side of the story. After it came out, I received positive phone calls from all over Iowa, saying how great my letter was.

James Flansburg wasn't the only opponent we had in Dallas County, but at least many of the others showed they had a sense of humor. At one public hearing, an anti-gaming minister stood up and said that people did not belong in casinos. They should be in church, he said, praying.

"With all due respect, Reverend," I couldn't help but reply, "there's a lot more praying going on in our casinos than in your church." Even the Reverend laughed at that.

I V

Bad media coverage wasn't our only problem, however. The city of Fort Madison tried to stop the *Emerald Lady* from leaving, claiming that we'd induced them to make riverside improvements and therefore owed them $2.6 million. But Judge Vietor rightly ruled against them. In doing so, he said that Steamboat Southeast and I had met all of our commitments, and had acted throughout "in utmost good faith." He ordered the immediate release of the boat and ultimately required the city to pay our court costs as well.

Meanwhile, an ambiguity in our agreement with the nonprofits enabled them to insist that we continue to contribute money to them, even after our boats had left. Also, because we hadn't given sixty days' notice to our employees, some complained that we owed them money under the Warren Act. Fortunately, Bob Ellis and Mike Sampson did a terrific job of settling both issues. They also dealt with our creditors, making sure that everyone was kept informed, dealt with fairly, and paid. I'd also like to acknowledge the support of our banks, who stood by us during this difficult period.

We offered all our employees jobs in Mississippi. One-third of them accepted. Those who didn't had little problem finding jobs in casinos in Illinois. If nothing else, we had given our people the best training in the industry. They knew their jobs, but more important they were always ready with a smile, making sure that our guests had a fun and exciting time. It hurt me that the newspapers said I didn't look after my employees. Taking care of our people has always been a priority at Alter Companies, and will continue to be so. One of my greatest pleasures and satisfactions of my success is the number of people I've been able to help to work over the years. Our scrap, barge, and casino companies have helped many thousands of people find work, build careers, and provide for their families.

Every time I go onto one of our boats, or even other people's boats, people thank me for the opportunity that they got through one of the Alter companies. Even today in the Quad Cities, I keep meeting people at bars, restaurants, and other places of work who got their start and their training on the *Diamond Lady* or the *Emerald Lady*. Many of them had been on welfare, living on food stamps, and now they have made good careers for themselves. They make a point of telling me how grateful they are for the opportunity that we gave them and that they have taken so well. There are hundreds of examples of careers that we started at Steamboat that are flourishing today. Recently, I was at a Quad Cities restaurant one evening, and two waitresses, Andrea and Annette, came up to me and thanked me enthusiastically for the training and the opportunity to work that the *Diamond Lady* had given them. Chris Walker is another fine example. He took a job as a security guard on the *Diamond Lady*, and when we moved the boats down to Mississippi, he spent his first days in Biloxi living in a tent, because he couldn't afford to stay in a hotel. Today, he is in charge of security at the Isle of Capri-Bossier City, one of the nation's leading riverboat casinos.

CHAPTER SIXTEEN
ISLE OF CAPRI

A strong theme is vital to a casino's success. When we moved our Mississippi riverboats to the Gulf Coast, we wanted a fresh, local theme, something that would capture the imagination and transport our guests to a whole different place. Then a Biloxi native told us the following story:

In 1925, Walter "Skeet" Hunt, William J. Apperson, and Arbeau Caillavet, three resourceful Mississippi entrepreneurs, had bought a small but beautiful barrier island, twelve miles off the Gulf Coast. The island, blessed with white beaches and large dunes and shaped like a panatela cigar, had just the one drawback: its name. "Dog Island" didn't exactly evoke the visions of paradise that Skeet Hunt felt it deserved, so he rechristened it the Isle of Caprice, pronounced Capri.

The three men spent lavishly, turning the Isle into a resort. They built a pavilion, restaurant, dance hall, and casino, luxuriously furnished with thick carpets, tapestries, and cushioned divans. A bathhouse, guest cottages, and beach cabanas were all connected by wooden walkways. A 600-foot artesian well supplied fresh water, and a small gasoline generator provided heat and lighting. Private boats and yachts moored against a 1,000-foot pier and dock. A floating rum ship allowed Isle patrons to forget prohibition for a while.

By May 30, 1926, the Isle was ready. Full-page ads in local and regional newspapers exhorted the public to "Join the Pleasure Throngs Where Ocean Breezes Blow," on the "Beautiful, Delightful, Colorful, and Gay Isle of Caprice." For the next five years, the Isle was one of the South's most popular tourist destinations, but the island's east end slowly eroded, and the Great Depression hurt business. Then, in January 1931, a fire set by some young New Orleans campers raged out of control, spread quickly to the other buildings, and burned the resort to the ground. All that was left of it was a sinking sandbar and the artesian well (which German U-boats reportedly used to restock their water supplies while lurking off the port of New Orleans during World War II). But by the early 1950s, that too had gone. The whole island had disappeared.

The moment we heard the story of the first Isle of Caprice, we knew it would be

START OF THE BILOXI--ISLE OF CAPRICE SWIMMING MARATHON BILOXI. MISS.

Postcard from the Isle of Caprice around 1930.

the perfect theme for us, if it was available. When we found that it was, our only argument was whether we should style ourselves the "Isle of Caprice" or "Isle of Capri." In the end, Boyce Holleman, a local lawyer, resolved the question by shrewdly pointing out that "Isle of Capri" has two fewer letters in it and so would be cheaper in light bulbs and electricity!

We decorated the boats in Caribbean style, with palm trees and bright colors and beautiful designs. It was fun and different, and it proved so popular with customers that when we later added casinos in other locations, we stayed with the same theme. Consistent theming worked well and made Isle of Capri a unique brand. We made other adjustments, too. We'd learned the hard way that we were a casino company, not an excursion company, so we installed state-of-the-art slots and redesigned the layout so that every possible corner of each boat was working productively.

II

Opening night at the Isle of Capri-Biloxi was a far cry from Steamboat's grand Bettendorf opening. For a start, we barely had two months to prepare, and that time was spent transforming our abandoned site in the industrial sector of Biloxi into a parking lot and dock. We relocated shrimp boats from their moorings, then sailed the two casino boats down from Iowa and moored them to a dock at Biloxi's Point Cadet, fixing them on either side of a converted barge. The local contractors worked through rain, weekends, and evenings to meet our deadline. We held a jobs fair, at which we were deluged with enthusiastic applicants. One in every ten Mississippi workers was unemployed at the time, and we were offering outstanding salaries, benefits, and promotion opportunities.

Opening day arrived. We offered no scheduled big-time entertainers, no excursions, only unlimited gambling. We waited anxiously to see how Mississippi would react to the new casino. After all, religion is central to Mississippi life, and some denominations had voiced their disapproval of games of chance. To our delight, however, we were mobbed by thousands and thousands of people savoring the fun. Huge lines formed outside, all the way back to the highway. It was a sweltering midsummer day, 95 degrees or more, and many Isle of Capri employees did nothing but shuttle out cold drinks and buckets of ice, like there was a fire to put out. Despite the heat, people stood in line for four or five hours for an opportunity at our slots and tables, not even sitting down for a while because they dared not risk their place in line.

The excitement didn't stop, but just continued throughout the night and the following days. The buzz of the gaming tables mingled with the humming of the slots,

The Ladies moored at Point Cadet, Biloxi, in 1992.

the clinking of jackpots, and the cries of jubilation. For thirteen days, the Isle of Capri was the only casino in the entire South, and it generated extraordinary interest and a cascade of cash. Our only problem was fitting our customers on board. We replaced our restaurants with banks of slot machines, and when that wasn't enough, we refitted the entertainment area with slots, too. In our first week, we took more than both boats had earned in a month in Iowa.

Within a month, a *President* boat and the *Biloxi Belle* arrived in town. Although both were crowded, our own earnings continued to be fabulous. In all my time in business, I'd never seen anything like it. In ten months, Biloxi profits had financed massive expansion and paid off our outstanding debts in southeastern Iowa. We didn't let our success go to our heads. We recognized that being in the casino business in Mississippi was a privilege, not a right, and Tim Hinkley, by now general manager of the Isle of Capri-Biloxi, worked hard for the local community. He became president of the Gulf Coast Chamber of Commerce, and, under his leadership, Casino America became the leading contributor to the United Fund in the whole of Mississippi. It also grew to employ 1,400 people and proved a tremendous source of jobs and wealth for the entire community.

And our pioneering leadership helped the whole Gulf Coast to astonishing growth. By 1996, Mississippi's gaming industry employed 27,500 people and paid $189 million in taxes. Welfare rolls were slashed and tourism boomed. In fact, the successful impact of gaming was so evident that Chevis Swetman, president of The People's Bank in Biloxi, was moved to remark that "We've had fifteen years of growth in the last two years."

III

With Biloxi established, Casino America began looking elsewhere for licenses and sites. We were not alone. News of the profitability of riverboat casinos had finally reached Nevada and Atlantic City, and the nation's leading gaming operators were starting to take note. Steve Wynn, Circus Circus, and Boyd Gaming were all keen to open riverfront and Gulf Coast casinos. We made a bid for a license in Tunica, Mississippi, just south of Memphis, but the gaming commission wouldn't approve our site. When Tunica became one of the largest gaming communities in the country, we thought we'd missed a wonderful opportunity; but in fact the resort overexpanded, and today Tunica has far too many slots chasing far too few coins.

But we did win a license in Vicksburg, Mississippi, and in 1993 we sailed the *Diamond Lady* away from Biloxi to Vicksburg and sited it beside a floating pavilion. (Her replacement at Biloxi was a permanently moored barge with two spacious gaming decks.) The *Ladies* hadn't proved great casino boats, but now they at least showed the value of their mobility. The *Diamond Lady* proved one of the great

The Isle of Capri-Vicksburg opened on August 1, 1993.

pioneers, too. Not only had she been the first casino boat to open in Iowa, she had also been the first to open in the South, and now she was the first in Vicksburg.

The Isle of Capri-Vicksburg opened on August 1, 1993, and soon expanded into a two-story, 32,000 square-foot Caribbean-themed floating casino, with twin cascading waterfalls, 773 slot machines, and 47 table games. It is about the prettiest casino anyone could hope to see.

Right next door, we added a 12,000-square-foot land-based entertainment pavilion featuring celebrity impersonators and other crowd-pulling events, and offering unbeatable value dining at the Calypso Buffet and Tradewinds Deli. Incidentally, I'd always believed that the restaurant business was about the last business I'd ever want to get into. I'd never dealt much with the public before Steamboat, and I didn't much like the idea of the long hours that restaurateurs had to work. Now, of course, restaurants make up a large part of our Isle of Capri business, and I've learned that the business and customers are tremendous.

We also added a 67-space RV Park half a mile from the casino, featuring a swimming pool, a spa, a guest services facility, and a free shuttle service to the casino. With Roger Deaton in charge, the casino did well. Our fortunes were on the rise, and so were our shares. Casino America stock had opened trading on the NASDAQ small-cap market in early 1991, before transferring to the NASDAQ National Market

System on May 11, 1993. In 1991, the stock price had been as low as 67 cents a share. Adjusted for a three-for-two stock dividend, by the fourth quarter of 1994 our stock touched its peak of $24.50 a share, and it has been on a roller coaster ride ever since.

I V

By now, Louisiana had also passed gaming legislation and had invited bids for licenses. We considered making a bid for a site in downtown New Orleans, but Elma Rosenfeld, my son Rich's mother-in-law and a New Orleans native, warned me that few locals would risk the gauntlet of downtown muggers to go gambling down there. She proved about the finest consultant I could have asked for, and cheap, too. The three casinos that did go into downtown New Orleans quickly lost fortunes.

We were more interested in Shreveport, Louisiana. The mayor of Shreveport was a Baptist and didn't believe in gambling. On the other hand, she was a pragmatic businesswoman and did believe in investment and job creation. Shreveport wavered a long time before allowing one license. Casino America was one of the three applicants,

The Isle of Capri-Bossier City opened in May 1994.

but I knew our hopes were doomed when Promus, owners of Harrah's and the Embassy Suite franchise, promised Shreveport a new City Hall as part of their bid.

Immediately across the river, in Bossier City, Louisiana, Edward DeBartolo Sr. feared that the new casino would severely hurt business at his racetrack, and he agreed to a joint venture with Casino America. Together, we lobbied for and won a casino license. The Red River at Bossier City was barely navigable, and we floated our casino boat as far upriver as we could, but then there was a drought, and it stuck on sandbank after sandbank. Our investment was marooned high and dry for two weeks, before thankfully enough rain fell for us to drag it to its permanent site.

But the shallow river had its compensations, and the legislators exempted the boats in Shreveport and Bossier City from cruising. That proved such an advantage that boats on navigable waterways also tried to stay permanently moored. They claimed minor obstructions in the river, excess wind, failing engines, fast currents, and all other kinds of excuses, until the gaming commission and the state police got tough with them, even inviting some of their top crew members to spend a night or two as guests in their police cells.

Isle of Capri-Bossier City was owned by the Louisiana Riverboat Gaming Partnership (LRGP), an equal partnership between ourselves and DeBartolo's local racetrack, Louisiana Downs. It opened in May 1994, with 62 gaming tables, 927 brand new slots and progressives, a 300-seat Calypso's Buffet and Coral Reef Grille, and a 100-seat entertainment area and lounge. It drew customers from all over Louisiana, as well as Dallas, just two and one half hours drive away. It was Casino America's third operation, and it became very profitable. We also acquired the 245-room former Hilton Hotel, three minutes' ride from the casino, and renamed it the Isle of Capri Hotel.

V

In 1994, pari-mutuel organizations in Florida banded together to put a constitutional amendment on the ballot. The amendment offered Florida voters a chance to license all dog tracks, horse tracks, and jai alai clubs for casinos. When Pompano Park Track came up for sale, 180 acres of quality property north of Fort Lauderdale between I-95 and the Turnpike, Casino America bought it for $8 million, with an additional $25 million payable if the amendment approving casinos was passed.

I thought that Pompano Park could make good money with the right management—Ted Snell as general manager, and my old friend and neighbor Jim Patten on the Pompano board helping Jack Gallaway and Allan Solomon. Pompano Park was a business opportunity in its own right, but it was also a magnificent site for a casino, if the Florida electorate so wanted. The vote was going to be close, and even if it didn't pass the first time, there was a good chance it would pass two years later. But the statewide advertising and public relations campaigns for the election were awful.

Casino America acquired Pompano Park Track at Pompano Beach, Florida, in 1994.

We should have promoted the good, fun news about casinos (increased employment, excitement, and tourism), but instead our advertisers brought up all the negatives, claiming that casinos wouldn't bring crime and vice and who knows what else to the area. It was a horror movie to watch, and it did far more harm than good. Around Pompano Park in Broward County, where we directed the campaign our way, the people voted in our favor. But in Florida as a whole, the amendment was crushed. Bad news followed when the Republican Party won the floor of the state legislature, killing our hopes of the amendment being successful in 1996.

Around the same time we were buying Pompano Park, the Crown Casino Group was issued a license for a small Louisiana town just to the north of New Orleans. They built a boat, fitted it with slots, and even hired a crew. Then the town changed its mind—they didn't want a boat after all. That left Crown with a major headache, at least until Casino America became involved. LRGP (our Bossier City operation) bought a half interest in Crown Casino and moved the boat to Lake Charles, where we had a license. Isle of Capri-Lake Charles opened in 1994, but despite our best efforts, it didn't do as well as we'd hoped. The trouble was, our boat had to cruise several times a day. Prospective customers could never be certain of getting on board right away, and others might be stuck on board longer than they wished, waiting for the cruise to end.

A local competitor tackled the problem head-on by securing two licenses, installing two boats, and shuttling them back and forth, so that one boat was always docked. Then, when the siren sounded to signal the start of a cruise, customers would simply pile their tokens into a cup and rush on over to the other boat. The idea worked, and the gamblers from Houston drove straight past our boat to get to theirs. As a result, our Lake Charles operation didn't come close to meeting projections. Before we'd even finished building the land-based pavilion, our boat was losing money. There was only one answer. We needed another boat and another license for Lake Charles, but as so often happens, the little cash we had to spare was being used elsewhere.

Our Crowne Plaza Hotel in Biloxi opened in 1995 and was promptly selected as Crowne Plaza Resort of the Year.

So many Biloxi and Gulf Coast casinos had opened up that Mississippi now had more casino space than Atlantic City! Some had built adjacent hotels and were offering enticing packages to attract people away from the Isle of Capri. As a result, business at our flagship casino had been slipping. We therefore built ourselves a 370-room hotel and opened it on August 1, 1995, three years to the day after the casino opened. It was, from the start, about the finest hotel in Mississippi. It immediately enjoyed 90-percent occupancy rates, was selected as Crowne Plaza's Newcomer of the Year, as well as Crowne Plaza Resort of the Year, and ranked first in guest satisfaction among the entire chain. Crucially, it also drew such

We opened the Isle of Capri-Lake Charles in 1994 and later added a second boat.

great crowds back into the casino that future expansion was soon being planned.

Meanwhile, in an effort to clear up our cash crunch and finance future expansion, Ed Ernst, Casino America's president and CEO, was thinking about raising $300 million through a public bond and stock issue. On the strength of that plan, he made an arrangement to buy the DeBartolo family's interest in LRGP for $125 million. To me, that was far too steep a price, but Ed insisted that it was the right deal, and he carried the board with him. Then the new Republican governor of Louisiana threatened to repeal the state's gaming laws and insisted that voters in parishes that already had casinos (including Bossier City and Lake Charles) have a chance to revoke the licenses. Such a loss would have crippled our cash flow, wiped out much of our investment, and, incidentally, cost thousands of local jobs.

The news created havoc with our share price and made a joke of our proposed bond issue and buyout of Ed DeBartolo. Thankfully, the board stopped the issue and the purchase. For this, and other reasons, Ed resigned. He had a noncompetition clause in his contract, but when he was offered the presidency of Casino Magic, a casino operator with casinos in Biloxi and Bossier City, we waived the clause on the understanding that he'd not try to solicit or recruit any of our people for awhile. Within seven months, several key Casino America managers had joined him at Casino Magic.

In December 1995, we got Jack Gallaway, a former executive of Sun International, out of his teaching post at the University of Houston to become our president. Rex Yeisley became our new chief financial officer, James Guay became vice president of marketing, and Tim Hinkley was later promoted to vice president of Casino America operations. He was replaced as general manager of the Isle of Capri-Biloxi by Bill Kilduff, who had also been with us in Iowa. With Robert Boone as vice president of human resources and Ed Reese as vice president of construction, our team was in place. The Casino America board of directors now consisted of Emanuel Crystal, Allan Solomon, Robert Goldstein, Jack Gallaway, Alan Glazer, and me.

We bought the *Grand Palais* from the New Orleans bankruptcy

Jack Gallaway joined Casino America in December 1995.

Emanuel Crystal, director of
Casino America.

Rex Yeisley, Casino America
chief financial officer.

James Guay, Casino America
vice president of marketing.

Tim Hinkley, Casino America
vice president of operations.

Ed Reese, Casino America
vice president of construction.

Robert Boone, Casino America
vice president of
human resources.

court, then submitted our request for a second Lake Charles license. The gaming commission was reluctant. We put on a presentation showing how much we had already achieved in the community. Leading local charities from Head Start to the NAACP, from children's groups to the United Fund, all vouched for the work we had done with them. It was excruciatingly close, but we won the vote. With permission granted by the state police, we put in our second boat, and now we always have one boat at the dock. Our numbers improved immediately.

We raised $315 million with a bond issue, paid off much of our previous debt, bought the DeBartolo family out of LRGP for $85 million, and bought Crown Casino out of Lake Charles. On November 5, 1996, we survived another threat, when all parishes in Louisiana with casinos voted overwhelmingly to keep them. The vote amply demonstrated how much benefit the riverboats had brought into their communities, even in a short period. A loss in Casino America's second quarter of 1996 turned back into profit by the third quarter.

We started working on adding new hotels in all our locations, and where we already had hotels, we began planning on adding more rooms. In September 1997

Artist's rendering of Casino America's Colorado venture.

Casino America opened a 240-room "Inn at the Isle" in Lake Charles. About the same time, in partnership with Nevada Gold (Casino America holding 58 percent; Nevada Gold 42 percent), we raised $75 million and broke ground for a new Isle of Capri Casino in Black Hawk, Colorado. In January of 1998 we broke ground in Bollinger City, Louisiana, for a 300-room all-suite luxury hotel.

The Colorado casino proved to be an interesting and challenging experience. Like a lot of other things, the casino business is about location, location, location. After the state of Colorado legalized casinos in three former gold mining towns (Cripple Creek, Central City, and Black Hawk), we, along with our partner, Nevada Gold, bought the best casino site in Black Hawk: on Main Street right at the entrance of town, the first casino folks will see as they drive in.

There was only one drawback to the site: it had a big mountain on it. Well, if it's a good site, why should this stop us? So early in 1998 we blasted 180 feet into the mountain and trucked away about 400,000 yards of rock and dirt (that's about 20,000 truckloads. To make sure nothing above the blast area slides down the mountain on us, we set about building a granite retaining wall and anchored it in firm stone using steel pins up to sixty feet long.

All of this cost us around $8 million, but it's worth it. Construction will be completed by January 1999, and it's going to be fantastic. We'll have a state-of-the-art casino: 50,000 square feet of casino and entertainment space all on one floor. Above that will be four decks of parking for a thousand cars, and above that a small hotel. The parking arrangement gives us a great advantage. People will be able to get out of their car in a dry building and enter the casino and hotel without going outside.

By the way, it will be our first casino not floating on water, which would have been pretty hard to do at 8,000 feet.

It turns out that there's an odd connection between our project in Black Hawk and the Alter family history. While I was out there visiting the site in the early stages of the project's development, I asked the city administrator how the city came to be called "Black Hawk." I was curious because, growing up in Rock Island, Illinois, I knew that Chief Black Hawk had also been a resident of Rock Island, about 140 years before me. The administrator went on to explain that the city had been a mining town, and a lot of equipment used for the mining operations had been from Black Hawk Foundry. Apparently, they looked at a piece of machinery that had "Black Hawk" on it and named the town after it.

Well, I told her, Black Hawk Foundry is located in Davenport, Iowa, and has been in the area as long as the Alter family. In fact, Alter more than likely supplied Black Hawk Foundry with the scrap that they used to make a lot of that machinery. So here I was, the better part of a hundred years later, doing business in an area that had held odd connections with our family for a long, long time.

With all these projects under way, things were looking up for us, once again.

V I

Through all our tough times with riverboat gaming, I'd never given up on my vision for Bettendorf, the Quad Cities, and Iowa. Illinois, Mississippi, Louisiana, and other states were benefiting hugely from the riverboat gaming bonanza, and I didn't see why Iowa, the state that had pioneered the industry, should do any less well. Yet the riverboat casino in Sioux City was struggling, and the *President* in Davenport was not making the anticipated returns.

Even as we moved our boats down to Mississippi, our attorneys continued to lobby in Iowa. Teaming up with the state's race tracks, which were also suffering, they campaigned vigorously for limit-free gaming. The Republicans had taken over the Iowa legislature, however, and they were instinctively against gambling. But then the public saw the *Diamond Lady* and *Emerald Lady* sail away, and they knew we wouldn't do that if we could make it work. They saw Robert Kehl's *Casino Belle* in Dubuque fail because of the restrictive limits. Now the *President* and the *Quad-City Times* finally changed their position, and started campaigning for limit-free casinos, and the public saw that gaming, instead of fostering vice and crime, offered jobs, prosperity, and wealth. They saw that Iowa people were taking Iowa money to Illinois boats, and they refused to put up with it any longer.

In 1993, the Iowa House and Senate finally removed bet limits and allowed as many gaming tables and slots as the boats could safely fit. Casinos still had to cruise, but the number of compulsory excursions was reduced to just one hundred a year. As soon as I knew the legislation would pass, I determined we'd return to Iowa and make good on our vision for Bettendorf.

At first, news of my return was unwelcome to local politicians, because many people still blamed me for leaving town. Several local councilors, while privately acknowledging I'd acted properly throughout and had had no choice, were still anxious about possible public and media reaction. They even threatened to take away our Bettendorf riverfront land and give it to some other gaming venture. But it was our land and our vision, and I stood firm. I argued the case for an Isle of Capri Casino-Bettendorf to the Casino America Board, but Ed Ernst, who was then still our CEO, didn't want any part of the new venture, believing the market would be too small and the publicity too adverse. The board turned the offer down. Instead, I offered the property and the chance for a license to other groups, as a partnership proposition on a 50/50 basis. Several groups were interested, but I insisted that any partnership would invest in land-based development, not just in a casino boat. As a result, only the Las Vegas-based Lady Luck group of casinos took me up on the offer.

Lady Luck was headed by Andy Topfitch, who began many years ago in Las Vegas with a small cigar store with a couple of slot machines and built it into a very nice downtown gaming establishment. When riverboat casinos were legalized in Mississippi, he put in casinos in Biloxi, Natchez, and Coahoma County. He competes

The Lady Luck Bettendorf *finally allowed me to make good on my vision for the Quad Cities.*

with us in Biloxi, only a few blocks away. Lady Luck has always run a good operation, and I've never minded the competition, because they're good competitors. Healthy competition helps everyone, and Biloxi is a prime example: after Las Vegas and Atlantic City, Biloxi is now the third-largest gaming venue in the country.

The Lady Luck group offered the added bonus of already having a casino boat under construction at the Bollinger shipyard in Louisiana, originally intended for another state. I had already learned that while our *Ladies* were beautiful, their casinos were much too small. I became increasingly aware that our customers were there to enjoy the slots and the gaming tables; if it happened to be on a boat, fine, but boating wasn't their interest. Few cared for the river views and atmospheric calliope music. We were, after all, in the casino business. Consequently, the boat being built at Bollinger met the requirements of what I felt a good casino should offer. At 100 feet wide and 300 feet long and sporting two decks, it was basically a big beautiful state-of-the-art casino that happened to have engines and would float. I wanted it for Bettendorf.

We set up a joint venture and leased our Bettendorf land and the boat to it. The boat did well from the start, employing locally, contributing to the local community, *and* making money. It lived up to all our original forecasts, and allowed our partnership to put in the $50-million land-based investment we had promised. Its success provided many millions of dollars for local charities, schools, hospitals, and civic improvements, at the same time it enabled further expansion.

Breaking ground for our new 256-room hotel in Bettendorf on June 23, 1997.

Lady Luck partnership (50 percent owned by the Goldsteins) broke ground on June 23, 1997, on a 256-room resort hotel, expected to open by September 1998. The hotel, with accompanying parking ramp and railroad overpass, represents an investment of about $25 million. The city of Bettendorf helped with a $7.5 million TIF bond for the parking building and railroad overpass. There are also plans for new restaurants.

Incidentally, I was the one labeled by the media as a man who cheated Iowa by not keeping his promises, while John Connelly was always feted as a local hero for promising $100 million. Our $52 million investment is already in place. With the hotel, parking garage, and overpass we'll have $90 million invested in the Quad Cities area, with much more coming. Where's Connelly's money?

Our Bettendorf casino was a tremendous boost to the whole community. Bettendorf companies found their business improving and land values rising. From about the bleakest depression in Quad Cities history, our casino initiative was finally helping lift the region back to prosperity. There was an interesting indicator of the impact of casinos on Iowans, too. The change in the legislation required ratification of casino licenses at the county level. Scott County, which had originally voted in favor of casino boats by a small majority, voted to retain them—but this time by an overwhelming margin, with over 80 percent of the voters in favor. Nothing could have made clearer that none of the feared evils had turned up during the four years casino boats had been operating in Iowa.

The riverboat casino industry in America began at 7:15 a.m. on April 1, 1991, when we launched the *Diamond Lady*. The more than eighty riverboats in America now employ more than 100,000 people, and along with gaming operations connected to Indian reservations and mountain casinos in Colorado, the industry continues to grow. I am proud of my contribution to the welfare of so many people.

CHAPTER SEVENTEEN
ON OUR METAL

While gaming was taking the spotlight (and the capital) away from our other interests during the 1990s, our barge line and metals businesses were both advancing well. Alter Transportation was now completely distinct from Alter Trading. It had separate offices, human resource departments, and ownership. It didn't even do much business with

Alter Trading any more. We moved most of our scrap on the inland waterways system in other companies' barges, and mostly saved our own barges for the more rewarding grain business.

By the mid-1990s, the surplus of barges on the inland waterways system finally eased, and that meant that at last the barge rates revived. In 1995, John McKenzie led Alter Barge to a bumper year, and in 1996 (in anticipation of growing business, and to preempt the gradual aging of our barge fleet) we ordered fifty new barges, with an option for more. It was our first order of new barges in fifteen years. In 1997, Jeff became president of Alter Barge.

Jeff Goldstein, my eldest son and president of Alter Barge Line.

*Rob Goldstein, my second son, succeeded Chuck Smith as
leader of Alter Trading Corporation.*

I I

Our metals business was also doing well, even though (or probably because!) I was no longer closely involved in it. Chuck Smith had retired in 1990 after his tremendous career, and my son Rob took over. He proved a great choice, not least because he was surrounded by a terrific team of people. Everyone from the janitor on up knew their jobs, and our most experienced people, like Jake Barnes, Art Petersen, Bob Pezley, and Bob Rosencrants, did everything they could to help Rob learn his. Like our other businesses, this area continues to expand. We acquired a new scrap yard in Norfolk, Nebraska, in 1990. We added another yard in Eau Claire, Wisconsin, in 1995. We bought Chanens' West Burlington, Iowa, and Quincy, Illinois, yards in 1997. In May of 1998, we bought a scrap yard in Grand Island, Nebraska, from the K.C. Nelson Company.

One of the new team's main ambitions was to build up our nonferrous business. In our scrap business, our reputation had been that of very good ferrous dealers and

Alter Trading's yard at La Crosse, Wisconsin.

Alter Trading's yard at St. Paul, Minnesota.

Our Council Bluffs yard still services Griffin Pipe, as it did thirty-five years ago.

Rufus Moore did great service to our nonferrous operations before his untimely death in 1996.

brokers, but we had very little reputation in nonferrous metals such as copper, brass, and aluminum. This was a challenge to us that we met when we persuaded Rufus Moore to come aboard. He had the know-how that we didn't, and under his guidance our nonferrous business mushroomed in both our yards and our brokerage business. He insisted that the quality we shipped to customers be perfect and with his help we instigated controls and sorting procedures that I would not have believed possible only a few years earlier. Sadly, Rufus passed away in 1996. Because Rufus was from Texas, the new 55,000-square-foot plant in Davenport that is dedicated to the sorting and preparation of our

Alter Trading acquired the Norfolk, Nebraska, yard in 1990.

nonferrous scrap for shipment is named "The Ranch." We now have one of the best reputations in the country for quality control, which is vitally important. As one of our customers once mentioned, if you don't really believe in quality control, just imagine yourself at 30,000 feet in an airplane, glancing out the window, and seeing the aluminum wing falling off!

Our booming nonferrous business allowed us to resolve another longstanding legacy of the Alter-Alloy split. In the mid-1980s, Alloy had finally gone bankrupt, leaving a real mess. The soil on its side of the Rockingham Road yard was contaminated with nickel, cadmium, lead, and other minerals, and the warehouse was stacked with hundreds of drums filled with all kinds of noxious cocktails. At Alter, we were not responsible for that contamination, but it was still a stain on the local landscape and on our family honor, too. I knew Frank would have wanted me to correct it, so we bought the property and began discussions with the EPA to clean it up to their satisfaction. It was neither cheap nor easy. Our first consultant advised us that we could clean it up for less than $1 million, but it turned out that he didn't know what he was talking about. We hired another consultant and discovered that our potential liability was far greater.

Then Jeff borrowed a cost-effective, EPA-approved idea from out-of-state, covering the affected areas with a special mix of concrete and earth, sealing in the contaminants. It was the first time the treatment had been used in Iowa, and it would have proved incredibly cost-effective and efficient, except that our legal and consulting bills more than doubled the actual physical cost! But at last, the steel wire fence came down, and the two halves of the Davenport yard finally came back together again, as Frank would have wanted. We turned it over to our nonferrous business, and now it is thriving again.

III

Rob and his new team were also making positive advances in other areas of our business, cutting costs and maximizing productivity. We added environmental controls for both water runoff and air emissions, set up strict source control programs, and insisted our suppliers document what they were bringing in. We installed state-of-the-art radiation detectors at all of our scales to ensure that we didn't accept any hazardous materials. We worked with Iowa's Department of Natural Resources on monofill regulations for the nonmetallic fluff of automobile scrap and constructed a state-of-the-art monofill for our Davenport shredder. We bought optical spectrometers to test the chemical composition of metals, then used metallurgical labs to confirm analysis, where necessary. The scrap business was changing rapidly, and I was pleased to see that we were still at the leading edge.

Customer service drove other improvements, too. We developed quality control systems compatible with our customers' needs. Because our foundry customers didn't want their working capital tied up in inventory, we improved our scheduling until our trucks could make a delivery three or four hundred miles away within a guaranteed half-hour unloading window.

But while our technology kept improving, the core of our business remained the same—building and keeping strong relationships by providing quality service. Sometimes that paid off in unexpected ways. Alter Trading had long enjoyed a strong relationship with the Inter Provincial Steel Company of Canada (IPSCO), one of the world's leading makers of steel. Then, in the early 1990s, they asked us to advise them on good sites for a steel mill in the United States from a scrap-buying point of view. It was smart thinking, because setting up in the wrong place could lead to unnecessary competition and needless costs.

We surveyed the entire inland waterways system for them, particularly studying the areas around Houston, southern Indiana, central Illinois, and eastern Iowa. IPSCO liked Iowa. They already had a pipe mill operation in Camanche, Iowa, and Governor Branstad made an impressive pitch to Roger Phillips, IPSCO's chairman. They soon found a perfect site a few miles southwest of Davenport. It was close enough to our yards that we could guarantee quality service, so we helped put their case to the state legislature, and agreement was reached. The new IPSCO mill soon began contributing to the economy of the entire region.

Even with this new business coming in,

Governor Branstad contributed greatly to bringing the new IPSCO steel mill to Iowa.

Rich Goldstein, my youngest son, is vice president of Alter Trading Corporation.

Alter Trading continued to stay loyal to its existing customers and vendors. Business relationships are two-way streets wherein you work with vendors and consumers in good times and bad times. This philosophy is what helps grow our scrap business.

With this and other new business coming in, Alter Trading was now a widely diversified and successful business. In fact, our success was placing a tremendous burden on our traders. While my son Rich was fast becoming a good trader, we wanted to recruit several more experienced traders, but their families often didn't want to move to Bettendorf, so we opened an office in St. Louis, which was a more convenient location.

I V

And that about wraps it up. As of 1998, Alter has been in business for a hundred years, and I'll have been in business for nearly fifty. I've loved every minute of it, including writing this history, which has given me a chance to reflect upon history, rather than try to make it. It has given me the opportunity to think back and appreciate all the good times I've had and remember all the good people with whom I've worked.

Thinking about history self-evidently forces you to look backward. But looking backwards can also help you to look ahead. After all, if you can see where you came from, it is often easier to see where you are going. As a result, I have found myself speculating over the past few months on where our companies may go over the next hundred years. I know making predictions in public can be a fool's game. I can't believe that when Morris and Harry Alter arrived from Ukraine, they imagined that their early efforts dealing scrap would one day lead to a barge line and a casino business! I'm equally sure our next hundred years will have more than one or two surprises.

Over the years I've learned that the future of your business depends upon and is often determined by how you define the business that you're currently in. One time I was at an American Landsman Association seminar, and we were asked to define our business. Now the scrap metal industry is commonly divided between dealers and

Casino America is in the fun business.

brokers, ferrous and nonferrous. But that clearly didn't define Alter: we were in all phases of the scrap business, much of which wasn't directly determined by scrap metal at all. Our trucks, rail, and barges, for instance, put us squarely in the transportation business, where we moved not only scrap but grain, salt, coal, fertilizer, animal feed, and other materials. Those activities put us in commodities, not only storing, handling and processing, but also merchandising and trading. Meanwhile, our ownership of the Blackhawk and Azalea fleets has gotten us into barge switching, customer loading and unloading sites, and more storage. We also clean and repair barges, do some dredging, and sell sand to the ready-mix concrete industry. That's a long way from just collecting and selling scrap metal.

The same is true for Casino America. By applying the same line of thinking—interpreting the real nature of the business you're in—it's clear we're involved in much more than providing places where people can do a little gaming. We're in the lodging business because we operate hotels in theme parks; we're operating restaurants of all types, and we're in the entertainment field as well. When you get right down to it, what we are really selling is fun. And the trick is to sell the customer a little better fun than the competitor next door.

What this means is that accurately defining what business you're *really* in opens up your thinking, because you're constantly aware that in two or three years your business could be structurally a very different company. Not just bigger, but structurally different. It's a daunting notion, in that elements of the company are never set in stone, but it's also liberating.

Our purchase of Pompano Park Race Track in Florida is an example. It wasn't a casino, but it fit our interpretation of ourselves as being in the "fun business." Given that definition, Pompano Park positions us to move in several directions. The race track already involves gaming, of course, and we know something about that. And should Florida legalize casinos, we'd be ready to adapt Pompano for that arena in addition to horses, giving us a terrific base in south Florida. And a track such as Pompano, with its decks and seating capacity, could also be a fine entertainment facility.

The same is true of our newest venture: cruise ships. Casino America very recently signed a joint agreement with Commodore Cruise Line to acquire and operate cruise ships. Casino America will also be managing the casino operations aboard Commodore's existing ships. Running cruise ships is certainly a different enterprise from operating casinos, but if one thinks of Casino America as being in the "fun business," it makes sense to move in this direction.

So, in both cases, defining ourselves more creatively helps us make more creative (and potentially lucrative) business decisions.

This kind of thinking makes it hard to predict the new industries we will get into (although if I were younger, the idea of building a passenger airline around our casinos would tempt me), but I will speculate about the future of the businesses we are currently in, and about the ongoing character and style of our company. All our businesses, the barge line business, the casino business, and the scrap metal business, have reason for optimism. None of them are subject to foreign competition, and yet there are opportunities overseas for all of them. In the casino business, people are going to have more and more disposable income, and more and more disposable time. They will be looking for excitement, and casino entertainment certainly offers that. We'll also have plenty of opportunities alongside our casinos. Customers will want their entertainment packaged together, so that they can golf and gamble, ski and swim, all in the same vacation. If we can provide them with that in a quality, customer-service, "Isle Style" way, then Casino America and the Isle of Capri have a terrific future.

Prospects for our barge business also look bright. Barge freight is the most efficient and cheapest way to move large loads. Waterways have less friction than roads, and therefore barges require less fuel per ton mile than trucks and trains, and less labor per ton mile. With the growing impetus for conservation, barge transport should certainly continue to grow. As for prospects in the Upper Midwest, there are going to be more and more people in the world, and all of those people need to eat. The most efficient way for the world to raise livestock is with Midwest corn and soybeans. God was good enough to put the right soil and the right climate by the Mississippi River, which enabled the Iowa/Illinois area to help feed the whole world and its growing population.

Mind you, however sophisticated our technology is becoming, it'll be a while yet before we can control Mother Nature. Corn and soybeans will continue to have good years and bad years, but thankfully for the barge industry, there are other commodities available. Our country is blessed with tremendous reserves of coal, and I am certain that coal will become a more and more important supplier of energy for those of our power plants within reach of our waterways. (I suspect that power plants remote from coal and cheap transportation will increasingly turn to nuclear power; oil will inevitably be reserved for mobile transportation until a practical substitute is found.)

The scrap metal industry will continue to use newer, more powerful technology, so that more tons will be handled more efficiently by fewer people. Consolidation will continue. We'll also see a wider range of materials being recycled. In a hundred years from now, at least half of the items that are now going into landfills will be recyclable. And the proportion of recycled material in new goods will increase. At the moment, although half of new steel comes from recycled steel, 60 percent of copper is from recycled copper, and 25 percent of aluminum is from recycled aluminum, only 10 percent of new paper products come from recycled paper. We'll also certainly find better ways to use plastics and old tires, for example, than burying them. Improved recycling will allow our precious natural resources to stretch further and further, as they will have to do.

I will make one other prediction. Despite all the things that will change, some things will stay as they always have been. The most successful companies will still be those that have the best people, that invest in customer service, and that do things on a timely basis—and with a smile. They will be the ones who supply their customers with more than they think they need, and their reputation will be vital to them. That is the reason for Alter's success in the past, and I'm a hundred percent certain it will continue.

How can I be so sure? From the first time Frank Alter went to visit William Butterworth, our people in all our companies have always done everything they could to deal with honor and integrity, and to exceed our customers' expectations. I know the new generations at Alter understand the importance of their customers, and will pass that understanding on to the ones that come after them, as I have tried to do. I also know that the old generations will be watching very closely what they're up to. They'll be looking down (or up, as the case may be!) to make sure that Alter stays in good hands. And that's why I'm sure it will.

I have just one final note. Frank Alter was born in December 1899, and my Dad was born a few months later, in February 1900. Alter Company itself was born in 1898, so we've really been tracking the twentieth century quite closely. I'll be expecting others to write Part Two about the twenty-first century and Alter Company's part in it. I can't wait to read it.

The Goldstein family today. Top row, left to right: Regina Feldman-Goldstein, Jeffrey Goldstein, Kathy Goldstein, Michael Goldstein, Susan Goldstein, Robert Goldstein, Marc Goldstein, Isabel Goldstein, Rich Goldstein. Middle Row: Samantha Goldstein, Joshua Millan, Bernard Goldstein, Irene Goldstein, Nathan Millan. Bottom Row: Alex Goldstein, Jeremy Goldstein, Lauren Goldstein, Jesse Goldstein.

ALTER TIMELINE

1898 Alter Company is founded.

1899 Frank R. Alter is born.

1900 Harry Alter arrives in the United States from Ukraine and travels to the Quad Cities.

1905 Morris Alter also arrives in the Quad Cities and takes work with his brother Harry, peddling scrap metal.

1907 Frank R. Alter arrives in the Quad Cities with his mother, Ethel, and sisters, Rose and Besse. Frank is seven years old.

1908 Morris and Harry Alter become joint proprietors of Davenport Iron & Metal, at 522 West 2nd Street.

1911 Davenport Iron & Metal moves to 425 East 3rd Street.

1913 Frank R. Alter starts working at Davenport Iron & Metal.

1916 Frank leaves school to join Davenport Iron & Metal full time. In the same year, he leaves that company to set up Davenport Salvage Company.

1920 Davenport Iron & Metal merges with Davenport Salvage. In the same year, Morris and Frank buy Harry out of the partnership.

The name of the company changes to Davenport Iron & Machinery.

1923 Frank Alter marries Yetta Gillman.

1928 The Institute of Scrap Iron & Steel (ISIS) is founded, forerunner of today's Institute of Scrap Recycling Industries (ISRI).

1929 Wall Street crashes, and the Great Depression begins.

Bernard Goldstein is born.

Frank Alter is elected president of Davenport Iron & Machinery.

1933 The company is incorporated.

1935 Davenport Iron & Machinery is renamed Alter Iron & Machinery Company.

1938 Alter Iron & Machinery Company becomes Alter Company.

1939 Morris Alter dies.

1942 The United States enters World War II. Within a year, the number of scrap automobiles in U.S. auto wrecker yards and scrap yards drops from 15 million to 400,000.

1945 Herman and Joseph C. Alter become partners in Alter Company. In 1947, they sell their shares back to Frank.

1947 Arant Sherman joins Alter Company.

1950 Bernard Goldstein starts working part-time at Alter Company. The following year, he joins the company full time.

1951 The Korean War increases demand for scrap.

Bernard Goldstein is elected secretary/treasurer.

1953 Chuck Smith joins Alter Company as a buyer.

1956 The city of Davenport decides to build a road through Alter's yard at 1701 Rockingham Road. The company relocates to the old Davenport Besler site at 2333 Rockingham Road.

Alter Waterway Terminal is established and begins operations on the Davenport seawall.

1957 Alter Company buys a Harris 3000 Baler.

Alter Company delivers scrap by barge to St. Louis for the first time.

1960 Alter Company buys the *M/V Frank R. Alter* and four barges, entering into the waterways transportation business.

1961 Gordon Jones joins Alter Company.

Alter opens riverfront yards in La Crosse and St. Paul.

1962 Alter opens the Council Bluffs yard, selling scrap to Griffin Pipe.

Alter Company begins selling to Mexico's Altos Hornos steel mill.

1963 Jake Barnes joins Alter Company.

Alter starts pushing grain down to New Orleans.

1964 Alter and Alloy split.

1966 Yetta Alter dies, age 62.

1968   Alter Eidal Corporation incorporated, using the name "Puremelt".

1970   Alter Fleet is incorporated.

1972   Alter opens its Des Moines yard.

1973   Frank R. Alter dies, age 73.

1975   Alter buys Newell Shredders.

1976   Alter Fleet changes its name to Azalea Fleet.

1977   River Rentals and Alter Truck Lines are both incorporated.

Alter buys David Solomon's yard at Dubuque.

First joint rail/barge bill of lading names Alter and Milwaukee Railroad.

1979   Alter Minnesota is incorporated.

Alter Metal Company is incorporated.

The Soviet Union invades Afghanistan, leading to the Grain Embargo, and a long recession for Midwest farmers and the barge industry.

1980   Alter acquires Rock Island River Terminal.

Alter acquires Builder's Sand & Cement.

1981   A brokerage office is established at Mobile.

Louisiana Scrap Metal Company is acquired.

1982   John McKenzie joins Alter Barge Line.

1984   Alter buys Des Moines Scrap Metal Company from Schwartz Group.

Dick Coonrod and Al Glazer are appointed Alter Company's first outside members of the board.

1985   Alter buys Cedar Rapids scrap metal company from Schwartz Group.

Blackhawk Fleet is incorporated.

River/Gulf Grain is incorporated.

1988   Green Bridge Company is incorporated and buys the J.I. Case Bettendorf property.

1989   Quad Cities Container Terminal is founded.

1990   Chuck Smith retires and is succeeded by Rob Goldstein as president of Alter Trading Corporation.

Iowa Racing & Gaming Commission awards riverboat gaming licenses.

1991   The *Diamond Lady* and the *Emerald Lady* are launched.

Builder's Sand & Cement is sold to Ira Weindruch.

1992   Casino America is launched. The *Ladies* sail down the Mississippi River to Biloxi.

1993   Isle of Capri-Vicksburg opens.

1994   Isle of Capri-Bossier City opens.

Casino America acquires Pompano Park.

1995   Lady Luck and the Goldstein family open their joint venture Bettendorf casino.

Jack Gallaway joins Casino America as chief executive officer.

Casino America opens Isle of Capri-Lake Charles.

Alter opens a scrap yard in Eau Claire.

1996   Fifty new barges are put on order.

1997   "Inn at the Isle" 240-room hotel opens in Lake Charles.

Ground is broken for Isle of Capri Casino, Black Hawk, Colorado.

Lady Luck-Bettendorf breaks ground for 256-room hotel.

Jeff Goldstein becomes president of Alter Barge Line.

Alter buys Chanens West Burlington, Iowa, and Quincy, Illinois, yards.

1998   Alter acquires a scrap yard in Grand Island, Nebraska, from the K.C. Nelson Company.

PHOTO CREDITS

INDEX

A genuine entrepreneur, Bernard Goldstein joined Alter Company in 1951 after receiving undergraduate and law degrees from the University of Illinois, and being admitted to the Iowa Bar. He served in turn as secretary/treasurer, vice president, president and chairman of the board, the position he holds today.

Under his leadership, the Alter Companies expanded from a single scrap metal yard into a major corporation. Today, the Alter Companies own a network of scrap metal yards across the Midwest, a significant scrap metal brokerage business, a substantial barge line, and other affiliated businesses.

Bernard Goldstein is also chairman of the board and chief executive officer of Casino America, Inc., which operates casinos in Mississippi and Louisiana, and Pompano Harness Track in Florida. He has been active in the development of riverboat gaming in a number of states and was instrumental in lobbying for the original gaming legislation in Iowa.

Mr. Goldstein, active in the community, created a Civilian Search and Rescue Fund and has received the Simon Wiesenthal Center Distinguished Community Award.